THE AMERICAN BANKING COMMUNITY AND NEW DEAL BANKING REFORMS 1933-1935

Contributions in Economics
and Economic History

THE AMERICAN BANKING COMMUNITY AND NEW DEAL BANKING REFORMS 1933-1935

Helen M. Burns

Contributions in Economics and Economic History, Number 11

Greenwood Press

Westport, Connecticut • London, England

Library of Congress Cataloging in Publication Data

Burns, Helen M
   The American banking community and New Deal banking
reforms, 1933-1935.

   (Contributions in economics and economic history,
no. 11)
   Bibliography: p.
   1. Banks and banking—United States—History.
2. Banking law—United States—History. I. Title.
HG2481.B85   332.1'0973   72-789
ISBN 0-8371-6362-5

Library of Congress Catalog Card Number: 72-789
ISBN: 0-8371-6362-5

First published in 1974

Greenwood Press, a division of Williamhouse-Regency Inc.
51 Riverside Avenue, Westport, Connecticut 06880

Manufactured in the United States of America

To my mother and father,
Helen and Harry Burns

CONTENTS

TABLES

PREFACE

This study traces the history of remedial banking legislation enacted during the period of the Great Depression. Two major themes are developed: the role of the banking community in determining commercial bank reform legislation, and the evolution of the New Deal banking policies.

During the Roosevelt administration, three major banking measures—the Emergency Banking Act of 1933, the Banking Act of 1933, and the Banking Act of 1935—were enacted. The first of these, the Emergency Banking Act of 1933, was born of the necessity of the hour. The banks of the nation were closed; their reopening, together with the restoration of public confidence, was essential. This measure achieved that end.

The Banking Act of 1933 was enacted during the first hundred days of the Roosevelt administration. While this measure is usually considered as part of the Roosevelt recovery program, it had only nominal support of the administration. The force of circumstances and public opinion played an important role in the passage of this legislation which increased federal supervision of banking and provided a guaranteed safety for bank deposits.

A study of the evolution of the New Deal banking program necessitates an examination of Franklin Roosevelt's outlook on banking. His views were crucial in determining the banking policies followed during his administration. Roosevelt sought the cooperation of the bankers, but the bankers feared what they believed to be the radical tendencies of his recovery program. Most bankers failed to recognize that the president, no less than they, was intent on preserving the existing banking structure. Nonetheless, changes in the banking system were necessary. Such changes were to be evolutionary rather than revolutionary. The needs of the overall recovery program and the desire of the administration to bring the banking system into step with the problems of twentieth-century America led to the drafting of an administration banking bill. The enactment of the Banking Act of 1935 concluded the bank reform legislation of the Roosevelt era.

This study focuses on those New Deal laws that applied directly to bank reform, and on the major financial legislation which resulted from combined political, legislative, social, and economic forces. It neither attempts to explore the myriad economic and social measures enacted during the Roosevelt years, nor to analyze the correctness or incorrectness of banking and monetary policies imposed during this period. In 1933 the stage was set and banking legislation was enacted against an already established climate. Therefore, little effort is made here to delve into the intricate realms of credit control and monetary management. Such topics are discussed only insofar as they relate directly to the consideration of bank reform legislation. Major attention is given to the commercial banking field; other areas of banking are considered only in their relationship to commercial banking. Finally, little attempt is made to trace the impact of the international aspects of the banking situation.

The opinions expressed in this work are my own personal views formulated on the basis of my independent research. The work does not necessarily reflect or express the opinion of any other individual, organization, or institution. Nevertheless, grateful acknowledgment must be given to the many people who helped in its preparation. Elizabeth Drewy and the staff of the Franklin D. Roosevelt Library were exceed-

ingly kind, as were James C. Brown of the Legislative Branch
and Leo Pascal of the Business Economics Branch of the
National Archives and Records Service. In addition, I extend
my appreciation to Powell Glass, Jr., the staffs of the Alderman
Library of the University of Virginia, the Special Collections
Division of the Butler Library of Columbia University, the
Manuscript Division of the Library of Congress, the Economics Division of the New York Public Library, and the
Federal Reserve Bank of New York. Special acknowledgment must be given to Professor Vincent P. Carosso for his
guidance and continuing interest in the work; he gave willing-
ly of his time and effort. To all others whose interest and
encouragement sustained me during this undertaking, I offer
my deepest gratitude.

THE AMERICAN BANKING COMMUNITY AND NEW DEAL BANKING REFORMS 1933-1935

Bank Reform, Remedial Action, and the Democratic Party 1929-1932

In the interregnum between the election of Franklin D. Roosevelt on November 8, 1932, and his inauguration as president of the United States on March 4, 1933, banking conditions throughout the country raced toward a chaotic climax. In the 1920s an epidemic of bank failures was symptomatic of the unhealthy state of the banking system. At the end of the decade the stock market crash of October 1929 and the depression that followed brought additional pressures on the banking industry and forced the closing of still more banks. As a result, the banking industry was subjected to rigorous scrutiny, and congressional investigations were held. As the number of bank failures continued to increase, public confidence declined and the faulty financial structure of an "overbanked" nation was strained to the utmost.

During the first two decades of the twentieth century, the number of banking institutions in the United States had rapidly increased. In 1900 there were 12,427 commercial banks; by 1920 the number had risen to 30,291 (see Table 1). Bank supervision then, as now, was divided between the federal and state governments. National banks were chartered by the federal government and were supervised by the Office of the Comptroller of the Currency. State banks were chartered by the various states and were regulated by the individual state banking authorities. In 1913, with the passage of the Federal Reserve Act, all national banks were required to become members of the Federal Reserve System. State banks, meeting the membership requirements, were permitted to elect membership in the system. In this way a new element was introduced to the dual banking system and an avenue opened to bring state-chartered banks within the scope of federal supervision. In 1900 the number of national banks totaled 3,731 as opposed to a total of 8,696 state-chartered banks. By 1920 the number of national banks had risen to 8,024. The number of state banks rose to 22,267, of which only 1,374 had joined the Federal Reserve System (see Table 1). In 1900 the total assets of national banks amounted to $4,944 million as opposed to a total of $4,115 million for state banks. By 1920, however, the assets of national banks had increased to $23,267 million and assets of state member banks of the Federal Reserve System amounted to $10,351 million. Assets of non-member state banks amounted to only $13,891 million (see Table 2). By 1920, therefore, although the total number of federally supervised banks fell far short of the number of state-supervised banks, a far greater percentage of the nation's commercial bank assets were subject to the surveillance of the federal government.

During this period, the growth of commercial banking was stimulated by the competition generated by banking institutions and banking authorities, both federal and state, in their attempt to provide banking services to more and more people. This resulted in overbanking and gave rise to a multiplicity of liberalized banking laws and regulations which were freely interpreted. As more and more banks received charters, bank supervision became lax and the way was cleared for incompetent management to gain control of numerous over-extended, undercapitalized banking businesses.

In the years following World War I, the American nation underwent economic changes that had direct impact on the banking industry. In the 1920s a consolidation and merger

Table 1.
Number of Commercial Banks in the United States, 1900-1936

Year	National Banks	State Banks		Total Banks
1900	3,731		8,696	12,427
1905	5,664		12,488	18,152
1910	7,138		17,376	24,514

Year	National Banks	Federal Reserve State Member Banks	Nonmember Bank	Total	Total Banks
1915	7,597	17	19,776	19,793	27,390
1920	8,024	1,374	20,893	22,267	30,291
1925	8,066	1,472	18,904	20,376	28,442
1930	7,247	1,068	15,364	16,432	23,679
1931	6,800	982	13,872	14,854	22,101
1932	6,145	835	11,754	12,589	18,734
1933	4,897	709	8,601	9,310	14,207
1934	5,417	958	8,973	9,931	15,348
1935	5,425	985	9,078	10,053	15,478
1936	5,368	1,032	8,929	9,961	15,329

SOURCE: *Historical Statistics of the United States: Colonial Times to 1957* (Washington, D.C.: Department of Commerce, 1960), p. 633.

Table 2.
Assets of Commercial Banks in the United States
(in millions of dollars), 1900-1936

Year	National Banks	Federal Reserve State Member Banks	Nonmember Bank	State Banks / Total	Total Banks
1900	$4,944			$4,115	$ 9,059
1905	7,325			7,217	14,542
1910	9,892			9,432	19,324
1915	11,790	$ 97	$12,219	$12,316	24,106
1920	23,267	10,351	13,891	24,242	47,509
1925	24,252	14,694	15,455	30,149	54,401
1930	28,828	18,521	16,776	35,295	64,123
1931	27,430	17,406	14,181	31,587	59,017
1932	22,318	13,538	10,448	23,986	46,304
1933	20,813	12,226	7,412	19,638	40,451
1934	23,854	13,529	7,595	21,124	44,978
1935	26,009	14,710	8,186	22,896	48,905
1936	29,643	16,881	9,048	25,929	55,672

SOURCE: *Historical Statistics of the United States: Colonial Times to 1957* (Washington, D.C.: Department of Commerce, 1960), p. 633.

movement took place in business and industry which resulted in a decline in the number of new banks established.
More important, however, was the impact of a decline in the
agricultural industry. In 1920/1921 there was a depression.
Business and industry quickly recovered and entered a period
of prosperity, but the effect on agriculture was prolonged.
In the postwar period, agricultural production had continued at the high levels achieved during the war, even though
the overseas demand for American food products had decreased and the consumption habits of the American people
were undergoing change. Consequently, chronic overproduc-
tion took place, the farm price index fell, farm income decreased, and bankers serving agricultural communities faced
tremendous pressures. Liberalization of the banking laws
had resulted in the chartering of a great number of undercapitalized banks in sparsely populated rural cities and towns.
As farmers defaulted on loans and mortgages and as deposits
declined, bank suspensions in rural areas proliferated. From
1921 through 1929, more than 50 percent of total bank suspensions took place in communities with populations of
2,500 or less (see Table 3), and more than 50 percent of the
failures occurred in banks with capital stock of $25,000 or
less (see Table 4).

In 1929 the stock market crash brought with it the end
of a period of securities speculation. The value of securities
declined rapidly and, although nonbank lenders had substantially swelled the volume of brokers' loans that contributed to the speculative frenzy of the decade, it was the
banking community that received the severest criticism. Investigations seeking to improve the banking system focused
the attention of the public on the interlocking relationships
between commercial banks and the securities industry. Moreover, these same investigations revealed more than a few
cases of lax supervision, bank mismanagement, and unethical
conduct. Public confidence in the nation's banks sank to a
new low.

As economic conditions worsened, pressures on the entire banking industry were intensified. The value of bank loans and investments declined rapidly as did the income of bank customers. Bank failures spread to the larger cities and the annual rate of bank suspensions was measured in the thousands (see Table 5). In the financial centers, runs on banks accelerated, hoarding of gold and currency resulted, and even the strong banks were dragged down by the cumulative impact of the panic.

As conditions continued to deteriorate, the expectation of an automatic restoration of prosperity faded. Bank reform was an important ingredient in the rehabilitation of the economic system. No longer confident of the bankers' ability to remedy the situation, the people looked to Washington. From 1930 to 1933, Congress considered bank reform legislation and the administration sought to rectify conditions through the cooperative efforts of business and industry. But the depression continued, the deteriorating banking situation gained momentum, and by March 4, 1933, the nation was faced with bank paralysis.

Throughout this period, the banking community itself was fully aware of the need for bank reform. Although some bankers urged unification of bank supervision under one authority, most bankers were reluctant to advocate measures that would greatly increase the amount of federal control over banking. State banking authorities opposed federal domination on the grounds that it was an infringement of states' rights. Among those bankers who did support bank reform there was little unity of thought on what was required or how it could best be achieved. The sentiment prevailed that bad banking could not be legislated out of existence. Reform, it was suggested, could be obtained by a stringent enforcement of existing laws and regulations.

The variety of institutions engaged in the banking business contributed to the complexity of the situation. There were

Table 3.
Bank Suspensions, by Size of Town or City, 1921-1929

Places with Population of—	Number of Suspensions								
	1921	1922	1923	1924	1925	1926	1927	1928	1929
Less than 500	189	136	313	316	218	372	259	199	235
500 to 1,000	99	59	118	161	125	218	148	97	139
1,000 to 2,500	82	77	114	136	129	208	126	106	137
2,500 to 5,000	36	31	33	66	69	70	61	31	49
5,000 to 10,000	25	17	23	31	30	32	17	24	35
10,000 to 25,000	30	11	14	28	24	24	34	17	24
25,000 and over	44	36	31	37	23	52	24	25	40
Totals	505	367	646	775	618	976	669	499	659

SOURCE: *Twentieth Annual Report of the Federal Reserve Board Covering Operations for the Year 1933* (Washington, D.C.: Federal Reserve Board, 1934), p. 222.

Table 4.
Bank Suspensions—Number Classified According to Capital Stock, 1921-1929

Banks Having Capital Stock of—	Number of Suspensions								
	1921	1922	1923	1924	1925	1926	1927	1928	1929
Less than $25,000	194	127	295	321	236	395	246	195	231
$25,000	107	90	151	190	140	233	167	107	151
$25,000 to $49,000	36	41	47	59	43	102	65	39	65
$50,000 to $99,000	83	56	92	124	131	167	121	96	120
$100,000 to $199,000	47	25	32	59	46	48	48	45	58
$200,000 to $999,000	16	15	16	16	18	15	15	11	20
$1,000,000 and over	3	------	------	------	------	------	------	6	11
Not available	19	13	13	6	4	16	7	8	11
Totals	505	367	646	775	618	976	669	499	659

SOURCE: *Twentieth Annual Report of the Federal Reserve Board Covering Operations for the Year 1933* (Washington, D.C.: Federal Reserve Board, 1934, p. 222.

Table 5.
Number of Commercial Bank Suspensions, 1900-1936

Year	National Banks	State Banks		Total Banks
1900-1909	118		375	493
1910-1919	82		579	661
1920	7		136	143

Year		Federal Reserve State Member Banks	Nonmember Banks	Total	Total Banks
1921	52	19	390	409	461
1922	49	13	281	294	343
1923	90	32	501	533	623
1924	122	38	578	616	738
1925	118	28	433	461	579
1926	123	35	766	801	924
1927	91	31	514	345	436
1928	57	16	406	422	479
1929	64	17	547	564	628
1930	161	27	1,104	1,131	1,292
1931	409	107	1,697	1,804	2,213
1932	276	55	1,085	1,140	1,416
1933	1,101	174	2,616	2,790	3,891
1934	1	-	43	43	44
1935	4	-	30	30	34
1936	1	-	42	42	43

SOURCE: *Banking and Monetary Statistics* (Washington, D.C.: Board of Governors of the Federal Reserve System, 1943), p. 283.

commercial banks, investment banks, savings banks, private
banks, savings and loan associations, credit unions, and the
postal savings system. The lines that separated the activities
of these institutions were not clearly defined; their operations
often overlapped and sometimes conflicted. Moreover, the
postwar trend toward consolidation and merger had resulted
in the development of group and chain banking, which in
turn had given rise to a growing demand for a more liberal
branch bank policy. In addition, an intimate link between
investment and commercial banks had been forged by
utilization of the security affiliate device. Superimposed over
this complex domestic picture were the repercussions of the
international banking situation which resounded in the financial capital of New York City and reflected down into the
local banking activities of each state.

Within the banking world, the division of opinion on the
question of reform revealed the numerous conflicts of
interest that existed. Some advocated a central bank, owned
and operated by the government, and opposed the regional
plan embodied in the Federal Reserve System. Another conflict focused on the problem of federal versus state control
over banking, an offshoot of the age-old states' rights question. There was also contention between large and small
banks, reflecting to a degree the problem of national versus
state banks, urban versus rural banks, and eastern versus
interior banks.

While the question of remedial bank reform was being
debated and discussed and general economic conditions
were continuing to deteriorate, the demand for action increased. In his annual message to Congress in December
1929, President Herbert Hoover had stated: "It is desirable
that Congress should consider revision of some portions of
the banking laws." He pointed to the competition between
national and state banks, and emphasized the problem created by the growth of chain and group banking. He suggested

that "it might be found advantageous to create a joint commission embracing Members of the Congress and other appropriate Federal officials for subsequent report."[1]

In the year that followed, Congress acted within the
framework of its own committee structure. On April 21,
1930, the Senate approved a resolution introduced the
previous year by Senator William King, Democrat from Utah.
The King Resolution provided for an investigation of banking
on twenty-one particular points.[2] This resolution was sent
to the Senate Banking and Currency Committee where it was
drastically amended, and a new resolution drafted by Democratic Senator Carter Glass of Virginia was substituted. The
provisions were broadened to provide for a complete survey
of the national and Federal Reserve banking systems.
Specifically, the resolution authorized the investigation of:

> the administration of these banking systems with respect to the use
> of their facilities for trading in and carrying speculative securities;
> the extent of call loans to brokers by member banks for such pur-
> poses; the effect on the systems of the formulation of investment
> and security trusts, the desirability of chain banking; the develop-
> ment of branch banking as part of the national system, together
> with any related problems which the committee may think it
> important to investigate.[3]

A subcommittee of the Banking and Currency Committee
was appointed to carry out this task. Carter Glass was designated as chairman. Hearings were authorized, a research staff
was assembled, and the results of the findings, together with
such recommendations for legislation as the committee considered advisable, were to be reported back to the Senate as
soon as practicable. To facilitate the work of the subcommittee, Senator Glass, on June 17, introduced a bill entitled
The Banking Act of 1930. This bill, according to Glass, was
offered as a tentative measure to serve as a guide for the
subcommittee's use.[4] In this bill, Glass, who had fathered

the original Federal Reserve Act, clearly defined the reforms that he advocated. The Banking Act of 1930 provided for restrictions on the security operations of national banks, the extension of branch banking, the regulation of security affiliates, the distribution of dividends on Federal Reserve stock, and the removal of the secretary of the Treasury from the Federal Reserve Board.

Interest in bank reform was equally intense in the House of Representatives. Pennsylvania Republican Louis McFadden, chairman of the House Banking and Currency Committee, stated that his committee would also undertake an investigation to determine the need for new banking legislation.[5] On February 3, a resolution calling for an investigation of branch, chain, and group banking had been introduced by Congressman Bertrand H. Snell, Republican from New York. This resolution was reported, debated, and approved on February 10,[6] and on February 25, hearings were initiated. Later during the session, a resolution providing for an investigation of the general banking situation was introduced by Chairman McFadden,[7] and as a result of his efforts the scope of the hearings on the Snell Resolution was broadened to encompass consideration of overall banking conditions.

The year 1930 was an election year and on July 3, Congress adjourned so that the legislators could return home to campaign. By June 11, the House Banking and Currency Committee had concluded its hearings on the Snell Resolution. New bank reform legislation still remained to be drafted. In the Senate the banking investigation was held over until Congress reconvened in the fall. Senator Glass expressed the hope that new legislation would be forthcoming at that time. Throughout the second session of the Seventy-first Congress, there was continued anxiety over the banking situation. Numerous bills dealing with banking matters were introduced. Some were ludicrous and were sent back to committee[8] where most of them died. Of those that did pass,

the majority dealt with the clarification of previously
enacted laws. Decisive action on overall bank reform legislation awaited the results of the investigations. At no time did
either house of Congress move to participate in the joint
commission to investigate the banking situation which President Hoover had recommended in his message to Congress in
December 1929.

Throughout this period the federal bank authorities—
the Federal Reserve Board, the comptroller of the Currency,
and the secretary of the Treasury—exhibited growing concern over the deteriorating situation; as the banking
crisis spread both the secretary of the Treasury and the
comptroller of the Currency pressed for legislation designed
to strengthen the banking structure. In his annual report for
1931, Secretary of the Treasury Ogden Mills pointed to the
weaknesses of the dual banking system:

> Our dual system and the divided control which exists have tended
> to relaxation in banking laws and regulations, and to the develop-
> ment of unsound practices in the management of the banks. More-
> over, recent events have disclosed as never before the extent to
> which many banks with deposits payable on demand have allowed
> too large a proportion of their assets to become tied up directly
> or indirectly in capital commitments. Furthermore, in some in-
> stances the functions of commercial and investment banking have
> become merged under the same management to such an extent as
> to present a difficult and important problem calling for remedy.
> These facts speak for themselves. The banking structure of the
> United States needs modification.[9]

In December 1930, Comptroller of the Currency John W.
Pole drew attention to "the failure of about 5,600 banks in
the past ten year period," indicating that these failures had
tied up deposits amounting to nearly $2 billion. This, he
believed, was responsible for the "crystalization of a strong
sentiment in favor of some change in our banking structure."

Emphasizing the number of failures that took place in rural districts, he recommended the institution of trade area branch banking for national banks, a measure which would enable national banks to disregard the geographic limitations of state boundaries.[10] His recommendation was supported by the secretary of the Treasury who saw no justification for the argument that banking should be confined to political rather than natural economic lines.

During this period the Federal Reserve System came under attack for failure to check bank participation in the speculative boom of the 1920s. Disclosures with respect to disagreements between the Federal Reserve Board and the Federal Reserve banks over open market purchases and the discount rate added fuel to the controversy. The recent appointment of Eugene Meyer as governor of the Federal Reserve Board had resulted in additional unfavorable criticism. The appointment was vigorously challenged on the floor of Congress by Representative McFadden, who strenuously voiced his objections to the appointment and seriously questioned the qualifications of Meyer for the governorship position.[11]

Although the legislative recommendations contained in the annual reports of the Federal Reserve Board for 1929-1932 did not propose major bank reform measures, the Federal Reserve System was greatly concerned over the deteriorating state of American banking. Two system studies were initiated: one dealt with branch, group, and chain banking and the other with member bank reserves. Both were matters of importance to bank reform considerations. Events moved too quickly, however, to await the result of such studies. Of greater significance was a recommendation made by Eugene Meyer (now confirmed as governor of the Federal Reserve Board) at a Senate Banking and Currency Committee hearing on bank reform legislation. Meyer recommended a uniform commercial banking system which would be achieved by limiting banking privileges to institu-

tions with national charters. At the request of Senator
Carter Glass, he obtained the opinion of the board's General
Counsel, Walter Wyatt, on the constitutionality of the proposal. Wyatt prepared a legal memorandum on the "Constitutionality of Legislation Providing a Uniform Banking
System for the United States" which supported Meyer's
recommendation. Although Wyatt's memorandum was
forwarded to Senator Glass, no move was made to include
the proposal in the bank reform considerations. Realistically,
it was unlikely that Congress would approve such a recommendation, for it would bring to an end the traditional
dual banking system in the United States. Politically, it would
be viewed as a disastrous encroachment on the inviolability
of states' rights.

   Although the Federal Reserve System did not offer a full-
scale program for legislative action on major bank reform, it
did pursue a policy of indirect pressure on banks in an effort
to stabilize economic conditions. In January 1931, George L.
Harrison, governor of the Federal Reserve Bank of New York,
indicated to the Open Market Policy Conference that the
banking situation had been of primary importance in the
recent reduction of the discount rate at the New York Bank.
He reported that, although he had been urged to issue a reassuring statement which might aid in quieting the banking
situation, he felt that such action was practically impossible
because if it were strong enough to do any good it would
risk contradiction by any small bank failure that might take
place. Nevertheless, he did believe that the rate reduction had
served as a method of telling the public that "money was
freely available."[12]

   During the first nine months of 1931, the Federal Reserve
credit policy continued to be directed toward furthering
easy credit conditions. Federal Reserve banks lowered the
discount rate and the buying rate on acceptances and made
additional open market purchases of government securities.

In the spring of that year, economic developments abroad
had an impact on American banking. In May a credit crisis
in Austria quickly spread to adjoining countries. As a result,
in late summer withdrawals of foreign gold balances from
London increased substantially and on September 20,
Britain went off the gold standard immobilizing gold balances
held in London and impairing confidence in gold balances
held elsewhere. The effect was that gold outflow from the
United States from the middle of September to the end of
October amounted to $725 million.[13] The external drain in-
tensified internal problems confronting American banks.
Hoarding of currency accelerated and bank failures increased.
The outflow of gold and the flow of currency into hoarding
caused the Federal Reserve banks to raise their rates on dis-
counts and acceptances. Reserve balances of member banks
decreased and there was a sharp increase in the volume of
member bank borrowing at the Reserve banks. During this
period, the Federal Reserve continued to exert persuasive
pressure on the banking community. Governor Harrison of
the Federal Reserve Bank of New York held talks with New
York bankers in which he recommended that the banks follow
a policy of very liberal lending, particularly to out-of-town
banks. He pointed out that this was a time when liquidity
should be used rather than preserved. Harrison reported this
to the Open Market Policy Conference in October. The
conference supported his stand and held that "everything
should be done to persuade banks to adopt a liberal policy
in this regard." Banks, however, were determined to preserve
their liquidity so that they could meet the demands of their
depositors. A rapid decline in bank loans and investments
resulted and credit remained tight. It was too late for persuasive pressure to alter the course to liquidity.[14]

From the White House, President Hoover, a staunch
believer in rugged individualism, endeavored to mobilize the
commercial community so that its members would help one

another. In October 1930, he addressed the annual convention of the American Bankers Association and stressed the
role of the banker in the recovery program. He called upon
them "to seriously and systematically consider what further
effective measures can be taken either in the business world
or in cooperation with Government in developing such
policies both for the present depression and for the future."
He said: "We have a need to consider all of our economic
legislation whether banking, utilities or agriculture, or anything else from the point of view of its effect upon business
stability." He called for cooperation, and said, "It is in this
manner that these problems should be met and solved."[15]
Ten weeks later, in a message to the final session of the
Seventy-first Congress, Hoover continued this theme. He
asserted that "economic depressions cannot be cured by
legislative action or by executive pronouncement. . . . economic wounds must be healed by the action of the cells of
the economic body—the producers and consumers themselves . . . recovery can be expedited and its effects miti-
gated by cooperative action."[16]

During the spring and fall of 1931, while bank failures
increased and large-scale currency withdrawals were made
by fearful depositors, Hoover persisted in his efforts to cope
with the situation by cooperative means. In August and
September of that year, bankers and businessmen met in a
series of private conferences at the White House. On
October 7, the president issued a statement which set forth
a definite program of action. He stated: "Our difficulty is a
diffusion of resources and the primary need is to mobilize
them in such a way as to restore in a number of localities the
confidence of the banker in his ability to continue normal
banking business." This, the president believed, would also
"dispel any conceivable doubt in the mind of those who do
business with him."[17] This drive for cooperative action resulted in the establishment of the National Credit Corpora-

tion, an organization to which the bankers in New York City made available, in accordance with the president's request, the sum of $500 million for the purpose of rediscounting for banks, when necessary, sound assets not legally eligible for rediscount at the Federal Reserve banks.[18]

The establishment of the National Credit Corporation brought a temporary reduction in the number of bank suspensions, and some currency flowed back to the banks. In December bank failures again rose and there were renewed withdrawals of currency. As the crisis deepened, the president sent his first message to the Seventy-second Congress. In reviewing the situation he was convinced that the economic system could be brought back to health without recourse to revolutionary action. As an emergency step in solving the credit paralysis which afflicted the country, he recommended the establishment of a Reconstruction Finance Corporation. This organization, conceived by Eugene Meyer of the Federal Reserve Board, was to be built on the lines of the War Finance Corporation of World War I. It was to have power to make loans, on adequate collateral security, to industries, railroads, and financial institutions which could not otherwise secure credit, whenever such advances would promote credit and stimulate employment.[19]

Hoover reiterated this recommendation on January 4, 1932, when, in a second message to the new Congress, he stressed that "the need is manifestly even more evident than at the date of my previous message less than a month ago." He emphasized the paramount importance of constructive action at the earliest possible moment, and indicated that his recommendation had been developed "in consultation with leading men of both parties, of agriculture, of labor, of banking and industry."[20]

The congressional elections of 1930 had increased the Democratic membership of the Senate, and, by a bare majority, had enabled the Democrats to take control of the

House of Representatives. Nevertheless, Congress cooperated with the president's request, and in less than a month, on January 22, the Reconstruction Finance Corporation Act became law. Upon signing the bill, President Hoover declared, "It brings into being a powerful organization with adequate resources, able to strengthen weaknesses that may develop in our credit, banking and railway structure." He stressed the fact that the RFC was not created to aid big business or big banks, since such institutions were able to take care of themselves, but, rather, to support "the smaller banks and financial institutions and through rendering their sources liquid to give renewed support to business, industry and agriculture."[21]

Within a month, a second emergency banking measure designed to bolster the sagging credit situation was introduced simultaneously in the Senate by Carter Glass and in the House of Representatives by Henry B. Steagall of Alabama, the new Democratic chairman of the House Banking and Currency Committee. This bill provided for the liberalization of the discount provision of the Federal Reserve Act so that additional bank credit could be made available. The measure, which had the president's support, was opposed by some members of Congress who feared its inflationary tendencies. Despite this opposition, it quickly passed both the House and the Senate and became law on February 27, 1932. Known as the Glass-Steagall Act of 1932, this was the first in a series of banking acts which would bear the imprint of these two gentlemen.

In his message to Congress on December 8, 1931, proposing the establishment of the Reconstruction Finance Corporation, President Hoover again called for remedial banking legislation.

> Our people have a right to a banking system in which their deposits shall be safeguarded and the flow of credit less subject to storms. The need of a sounder system is plainly shown by the extent of

bank failures. I recommend the prompt improvement of the banking laws. Changed financial conditions and commercial practices must be met. The Congress should investigate the need for separation between different kinds of banking; an enlargement of branch banking under proper restriction; and the methods by which enlarged membership in the Federal reserve system may be brought about.[22]

The Senate Banking and Currency Committee investigation authorized in 1930 continued throughout 1931. During 1931 hearings were held. Leading members of the banking fraternity gave testimony, extensive studies were made by the subcommittee staff, and pertinent information was obtained from the federal banking agencies and the Federal Reserve banks. The work undertaken constituted the most comprehensive investigation of the general banking situation since that done by the National Monetary Commission in 1908.

Although the final session of the Seventy-first Congress adjourned on March 4, 1931, the Glass subcommittee continued its work of gathering and assessing information so that a bank reform bill would be ready for the new Congress. This measure, the outgrowth of the hearings and studies of the previous year, was introduced in the Senate by Carter Glass on January 21, 1932. Its introduction was greeted with an immediate outburst of opposition from members of the administration, the banking community, and Congress. After Glass conferred with Hoover, the measure was redrafted by the Banking and Currency Committee and was introduced under a new bill number on March 17. Opposition continued and additional redrafting took place. This resulted in a third bill which was introduced on April 18.[23] The passage of this bill through the Senate was to be long and stormy. It was eventually approved and sent to the House of Representatives where, in the final days of the Hoover administration, it was laid to rest in the House Banking and Currency Committee.

A flood of legislation purporting to remedy the banking situation engulfed the first session of the Seventy-second Congress. Few bills achieved passage; most died in committee. One topic predominated: the guaranteed safety for bank depositors' funds. The overwhelming number of bank failures had wrought severe hardship on bank depositors. Concern for their plight was of prime importance to the legislators, as is reflected in the introduction of more than twenty bills on this subject. Members of both parties and representatives from diverse sections of the country claimed sponsorship. Neither special interests nor regional implications characterized the support for these measures.

Of the bills introduced, attention centered primarily on a measure presented by Congressman Steagall on April 14, 1932.[24] This bill provided for a guarantee fund for deposits in banks. It covered national banks, Federal Reserve member banks, and nonmember state banks. The Steagall bill was to be vigorously debated on the floor of Congress, in banking journals, and in the general press. Bankers in particular were opposed to its enactment. Government officials pointed in alarm to the failure of similar plans instituted at the state level. The general public, however, dismayed by the growing number of bank failures, looked with favor on the prospect of guaranteed safety for bank deposits. The bill was sent to the House Banking and Currency Committee, reported out, and was discussed at length on the floor of the House. On May 27, it passed the House with amendments. On May 29, it was sent to the Senate where it was referred to the Senate Banking and Currency Committee. There it remained until the close of the final session of the Seventy-second Congress.

While Congress considered remedial banking legislation, the Reconstruction Finance Corporation began operation. A decline in bank failures resulted. *Time* magazine indicated that the number of suspensions for April had been reduced

to 68 as opposed to the all-time high of 522 reported in
October 1931.[25] Nevertheless, currency hoardings continued and the credit situation did not ease. The administration inaugurated an anti-hoarding campaign. Frank Knox,
editor of the *Chicago Daily News*, was named to head a
Citizens Reconstruction Organization and in March it was
reported that that organization would conduct a house-to-
house-canvas to get people to spend or invest money.[26]

It was not only private hoarding which concerned the
administration. Bankers, the White House believed, were also
hoarding. Earlier in the year, in an address before the American Acceptance Council, Secretary of the Treasury Ogden
Mills stated that bankers could take definite corrective
steps in relation to the movement of bank deposits. He held
that "a direct responsibility rests on the great banking institutions of the country . . . they must establish a solid front
and through a cooperative and unified program attack a
problem that they above all others are best fitted to solve."[27]
Letters flooded the president's desk telling of loans denied,
on what borrowers considered adequate collateral. A sampling
of such letters which Hoover sent to Governor Harrison reflected the strong public feeling against the bankers. In his
covering letter the president wrote, "I can see a rising tide
toward the banks which is going to be perfectly disastrous
unless we can secure better cooperation." In reply, Harrison
expressed his surprise that "so much of the feeling prevailed
with respect to the banks located outside New York City,
where so much of the criticism has been concentrated."
Harrison felt that there were signs that the Reserve System's
open market purchases of government securities would relax
the attitude of many banks. He pointed out, however, that
the confused legislative situation in Washington would deter
the banks from an active response to Reserve bank policy.[28]

In 1932 the easy money policy of the Federal Reserve
System enabled member banks to meet the demands made

upon them for gold and currency and to reduce their indebtedness at the Federal Reserve banks. Although a considerable volume of excess reserves accumulated, bank credit
remained tight. In a letter to the president of Bankers Trust
Company in New York, Ogden Mills observed: "I cannot help
but feel that part, at least, of the contraction of bank credit
during the last three or four months has been brought about
by what I called the psychology of fear which has affected
bankers quite as much as their depositors." Mills believed
that money conditions could not be eased until "the predominant impulse among banks was to put their resources
to work rather than conserving them at all costs."[29]

In May the Federal Reserve took steps to actively enlist
the cooperation of bankers and businessmen in developing
ways for making effective use of the funds being made
available by the open market operations of the Federal
Reserve System. Banking and industrial committees composed of businessmen and bankers were set up in each
Federal Reserve district. These committees conducted surveys to ascertain to what extent the legitimate credit requirements of commerce, industry, and agriculture were not
being supplied because of a lack of banking facilities or for
other reasons, and to acquaint prospective borrowers with
possible sources of credit. In many instances it was possible
to establish contact between prospective borrowers and
the appropriate lending agencies. But bank credit at commercial banks remained unobtainable for all except borrowers
of the highest credit rating. Banks were willing to risk only
the most conservative of loans. The recent gold and currency
drains and the ever-increasing number of bank failures motivated them toward liquidity and self-preservation.

While the administration endeavored to loosen the tight
credit situation and provide for the expansion of bank loans,
other forces were at work within Congress which would have
an additional impact on the banking crisis. The White House

believed that the increased amount of short selling in the
securities market was destroying public confidence in the
economy. Hoover, therefore, gave his support to a resolution
introduced in the Senate which called for an investigation of
short selling of listed securities on the numerous exchanges.
The president had no thought of a detailed probe into the
entire Wall Street structure. Even so, the investigation was
broadened and a thorough and complete probe of stock
market practices was authorized so that the Senate could
determine whether such practices should be regulated. Hearings were held and witnesses were summoned to Washington
to answer embarrassing questions. As the investigations
progressed, it became evident that many bankers had been
somewhat less than altruistic in their efforts to halt the
depression, that they had in fact taken advantage of the
situation to unload worthless securities on unsuspecting in-
vestors. Public resentment against the bankers increased.

Meanwhile, in the House of Representatives a third emergency measure designed to accompany the RFC and the Glass-
Steagall Act was sponsored by T. Alan Goldsborough, Democrat from Maryland. This bill required the Federal Reserve
System to take all available steps to raise deflated com-
modity prices to their pre-depression level.[30] How this was
to be accomplished was not precisely defined. The measure
was opposed by the Federal Reserve authorities and by the
president. It gained Democratic party support and passed
the House under Democratic sponsorship. In the Senate,
however, opposition from Democratic Senator Carter Glass
dealt a death blow to the measure when it was referred to
the Senate Banking and Currency Committee.

Cooperation between the White House and Capitol Hill
continued to deteriorate. Upon signing the Reconstruction
Finance Corporation Act, the president had emphasized
that it was created to aid the small banks. Within a few
months widespread rumors that RFC loans were being made

to large banks sowed doubts as to the truth of that statement. These suspicions were confirmed when it became public knowledge that $90 million had gone to the Central Republic Bank of Chicago, headed by Charles G. Dawes, who had himself recently resigned from the presidency of the RFC. The legislators were incensed. Shortly thereafter Congress passed an amendment requiring the corporation to make monthly reports to the president, the Senate, and the House of Representatives on all loans granted during the previous month.[31] The new law did not require that this information be publicized, but Speaker of the House John Nance Garner instructed the Clerk of the House to release the reports. The Democrats made political capital of the fact that, although a greater number of loans went to small banks, a greater percentage of money went to large banks. Publication of this information was strenuously protested by the administration and by the Reconstruction Finance Corporation. But the practice continued. Efforts at nonpartisan action came to an end on Capitol Hill.

Conditions were bad and were rapidly growing worse, when in the summer of 1932 the nation turned to the quadrennial task of electing a president. The depression was the key issue of the campaign and the unsettled banking situation inevitably became involved in politics. Hoover stood for reelection, and was opposed by Franklin Delano Roosevelt, the personable governor of New York. Hoover's views on bank reform were well known. The record of his administration and his addresses to Congress marked him as a conservative in banking and on monetary matters. The views of his opponent were less clear.

The platform adopted by the Democratic party contained planks pertaining to banking. It stated:

> We advocate quicker methods of realizing on assets for the relief
> of depositors of suspended banks, and a more rigid supervision

of national banks for the protection of depositors and the pre-
vention of the use of their moneys in speculation to the detriment
of local credits.

The severance of affiliated security companies from and the divorce
of the investment banking business from commercial banks and
further restrictions of Federal reserve banks in permitting the use
of Federal reserve facilities for speculative purposes.[32]

These planks reflected the division of opinion that existed
within the Democratic party itself on the question of bank
reform. Carter Glass, who drafted this section of the platform, had successfully opposed the inclusion of any support
for deposit guaranty plans. However, he was unable to gain
party endorsement for the Glass banking bill, and the question of unification of the banking system under federal law
was completely ignored.

In his speech accepting his party's nomination, Franklin
Roosevelt adopted this platform in its entirety. Later in the
campaign, in an address delivered at Columbus, Ohio, he
reasserted his support of those planks directly pertaining to
banking when, in enumerating needed reforms, he advocated
the following:

Fourth—The events of the past three years prove that the supervision of national banks for the protection of the public has been
ineffective. I propose vastly more rigid supervision.

Fifth—We have witnessed not only the unrestricted use of bank
deposits in speculation to the detriment of local credit, but we are
also aware that this speculation was encouraged by the Government
itself. I propose that such speculation be discouraged and prevented.

Sixth—Investment banking is a legitimate business. Commercial
banking is another wholly separate and distinct business. Their consolidation and mingling are contrary to public policy. I propose their
separation.

Seventh—Prior to the Panic of 1929 the funds of the Federal Reserve

System were used practically without check for many speculative
enterprises. I propose the restrictions of Federal Reserve Banks in
accordance with the original plans and earlier practices of the
Federal Reserve System under Woodrow Wilson.[33]

The outcome of the election gave the nation a lame duck
president. In December 1932 the last lame duck session of
the Congress was to assemble. With the results of the election
in mind, banking authorities conferred on what steps to take
during the period of transition. Governor Harrison talked
with Secretary of the Treasury Mills and urged that a program for nonpartisan action in Congress be formulated. He
raised the question of whether it might not be appropriate
to call in "leaders of both parties as soon as possible to formulate a program designed to reach some common opinion on
economy, taxes, the budget, war debts, banking legislation,
etc." Harrison believed this question to be of vital importance
if "we are to avoid retrogression in the next four months
pending the inaugration of the new administration." Mills,
sharing this view, asserted that "if the Democrats are wise
they will get busy at once if they want to avoid a much
worse situation when they take office in March." He felt it
would be impossible for the Republicans to take leadership
in the next four months. He pointed to the Democratic
strength in Congress and said that "the Democrats cannot
avoid the responsibility of leadership between now and
March 4." He thought "it would probably be taken amiss
by the Democrats "if the Republicans tried to take leadership
now."[34]

On December 6, in his last report on the State of the
Union, President Hoover made a final plea for banking
legislation, emphasizing that "widespread banking reforms
are a national necessity and are the first requisites for further recovery."[35] The Democrats, already in control of the
House and looking forward to March when they would control both chambers of Congress, had little inclination to

cooperate with the Republican administration. In the
Senate, Carter Glass continued to press for the passage of
his banking bill. Although many who had originally opposed the measure now gave it support, others held that the
times were too perilous and that a bank reform bill with extensive ramifications should not be considered as an emergency measure. The opposition gained unexpected support
when the bill came up for debate in the Senate. In a filibuster
which lasted for more than a week, Huey Long, the junior
senator from Louisiana, fought vehemently against the
branch banking provision of the Glass bill, asserting that it
would concentrate power in the hands of a few institutions
and would harm local communities. On January 25, when
the bill came up for final vote, he summed up his position:

> I am glad to say we have painted this bill as it should have been
> painted. I am glad to say that it has no more chance of becoming
> a law than I have of becoming Pope of Rome, and I am a Baptist.
> I wish to say that it does not make any difference now what hap-
> pens here, we have dressed it up and crippled it in this iniquitous
> body, and I do not think it can hobble through another proceeding
> of any kind or character.[36]

Following the Long filibuster, the Glass bill was passed and
sent to the House of Representatives, where it was promptly
relegated to the Banking and Currency Committee for study.
In the interim, while the Senate had debated the Glass bill,
the House passed a resolution which demanded that the
RFC report all loans made since the corporation's incep-
tion.[37] As had been true of the monthly reports, the additional information was now made public knowledge.

While the administration and Congress continued to disagree, the shadows of disaster lengthened. Since the first
days of the depression, local bank moratoria had been utilized to aid banks facing runs. This was usually done through
the declaration of a holiday. In November, Nevada employed

this device, declaring a statewide holiday. In Louisiana early in the new year, the governor declared a holiday ostensibly to celebrate the day President Wilson gave the German ambassador his walking papers. On February 14, Governor William Comstock of Michigan closed the banks in his state.

In New York George L. Harrison kept in close touch with the deepening crisis. He conferred with Owen D. Young, deputy chairman of the New York Federal Reserve Bank, and with William Woodin, a director of the New York Bank and a staunch Roosevelt supporter. The three men discussed the advisability of a conference with Roosevelt to inform him of the facts of the banking situation so that there would be no question later about his having been ignorant of developments. Acting as intermediary, William Woodin brought back from Roosevelt's headquarters a request for a memorandum of conditions as Harrison saw them. Harrison was reluctant to comply as he believed some things should not be put in writing. Instead, he proposed that Roosevelt should immediately appoint his secretary of the Treasury and issue a statement expressing his position on a balanced budget and sound currency. Harrison believed such action would do more than anything else to allay fears both at home and abroad.[38]

Meanwhile, in Detroit, federal banking authorities, eminent bankers, and local government officials endeavored to ease conditions, and from the White House Herbert Hoover sent to his successor a ten-page handwritten letter in which he described the seriousness of the situation. He urged the president-elect to issue a statement:

> The major difficulty is the state of the public mind for there is a steadily degenerating confidence in the future which has reached the height of general alarm. I am convinced that a very early statement by you upon two or three policies of your Administration would greatly serve to restore confidence and cause a resumption of the march of recovery.[39]

In New York, Franklin Roosevelt was busy gathering together his new administration. Negotiations were underway regarding cabinet appointments. The problems of the depression were under consideration by the "Brain Trust." The president-elect, fresh from his southern vacation, was enigmatic about his plans to cope with the deteriorating banking situation. In reply to the president's letter he wrote:

> I am equally concerned with you in regard to the gravity of the present bank situation—but my thought is that it is so very deep-seated that the fire is bound to spread in spite of anything that is done by mere statement. The real trouble is that on present values very few financial institutions anywhere in the country are actually able to pay off their deposits in full, and the knowledge of this fact is widely held.[40]

No statement was issued. In New York, Detroit, Chicago, and other financial centers around the country, bankers and government officials gathered to cope with the disastrous situation. Moratoria spread. In Indiana on February 23, in Maryland on February 25, in Arkansas on February 27, and in Ohio on February 28, bank holidays were declared.[41] The economic heartbeat of the nation was slowing to a standstill. The outgoing administration was reluctant to act independently, and the incoming administration felt it could not act cooperatively. All studies, investigations, commissions, as well as bankers and Congress had failed; in the Senate and the House of Representatives remedial banking legislation lay buried in committee.

NOTES

1. *Congressional Record,* 116 vols. (Washington, D.C., 1873) LXXII, p. 25.
    2. Ibid., LXXI, p. 2322.

3. Ibid., LXXII, p. 83355.

4. Ibid., p. 10973.

5. *The New York Times*, January 8, 1930.

6. *Congressional Record*, LXXII, p. 3383.

7. Ibid., LXXIV, p. 1901.

8. H.R. 9683 was introduced by Charles Brand, Democrat from Georgia. It prohibited the circulation of false rumors about banks (*Congressional Record*, LXXII, p. 3331). It was amended by Edgar Howard, Democrat from Nebraska, to make it illegal for bankers to circulate false reports about citizens (*Congressional Record*, LXXII, pp. 4828-4820). Brand then declared the bill had been made a monstrosity and requested its return to committee (*Congressional Record*, LXXII, p. 3331; *The New York Times*, March 6, 1930).

9. U.S. Secretary of the Treasury, *Annual Report, June 30, 1931* (Washington, D.C., 1932), p. 32.

10. U.S. Comptroller of the Currency, *Annual Report, December 1, 1930* (Washington, D.C., 1931), p. 1.

11. Governor Roy B. Young of the Federal Reserve Board resigned to become governor of the Federal Reserve Bank of Boston. Simultaneously, Vice-Governor Edmund Platt resigned to become vice-president of the Marine Midland Group of banks. McFadden asserted that these changes had been contrived to clear the way for Meyer's appointment. In addition, McFadden charged that Meyer was closely connected with banking houses of international reputation. He stated: "If you want to turn the Federal Reserve System over to international financiers place Mr. Meyer in that particular post at this time." *Congressional Record*, LXXVI, pp. 2835, 4352.

12. Federal Open Market Policy Conference, Minutes of Meeting, January 21, 1931, 3 vols., II, George L. Harrison Papers, Butler Library, Columbia University. (Hereafter referred to as Harrison Papers.)

13. Federal Reserve Bank of New York, *Seventeenth Annual Report for Year Ending December 31, 1931* (New York, 1932), p. 13.

14. Federal Open Market Policy Conference, Minutes of Meeting, October 26, 1931, II, Harrison Papers.

15. William S. Meyer, ed., *The State Papers and Other Public Writings of Herbert Hoover*, 2 vols. (Garden City, N.Y., 1934), I, pp. 375-384; *Congressional Record*, LXXIV, pp. 202-203.

16. Ibid., p. 33.

17. Meyer, *The State Papers and Other Public Writings of Herbert Hoover*, II, pp. 4-7; Federal Reserve Board, *Federal Reserve Bulletin* (Washington, D.C., 1932), pp. 551-553.

18. Ibid.

19. *Congressional Record*, LXXV, p. 25.

20. Ibid., p. 1157.

21. Meyer, *The State Papers and Other Public Writings of Herbert Hoover*, II, pp. 106-107.

22. *Congressional Record*, LXXV, p. 25.

23. X.3215 was introduced on January 21, 1932, *Congressional Record,* LXXV, p. 2403; S.4115 was introduced on March 17, 1932, ibid., p. 6329; S.4412 was introduced on April 18, 1932, ibid., p. 8350.

24. Ibid., p. 8273.

25. *Time,* XIX (May 30, 1932), p. 12.

26. Ibid. (March 14, 1932), p. 5.

27. Ogden L. Mills, *Credit and Confidence, An Address . . . at the Annual Meeting of the American Acceptance Council,* January 25, 1932 (New York, 1932), pp. 5, 10.

28. Hoover to Harrison, April 26, 1932, and Harrison to Hoover, May 3, 1932. Personal Correspondence, Hoover Folder, Harrison Papers.

29. Ogden L. Mills to Guy Emerson, March 12, 1932. Ogden L. Mills Papers, Container 110, Library of Congress.

30. Ibid., p. 8346.

31. Ibid., pp. 14489-15491.

32. *The New York Times,* June 30, 1932; *Congressional Record,* LXXV, p. 14735.

33. Samuel I. Rosenman, Comp., *The Public Papers and Addresses of Franklin D. Roosevelt,* 13 vols. (New York, 1938-1950), I, pp. 682-683.

34. Summary of telephone conversation between Harrison and Mills, November 10, 1932, Harrison to Confidential Files, November 12, 1932, "Conversations," Harrison Papers.

35. *Congressional Record,* LXXV, p. 53.

36. Ibid., p. 2508.

37. Ibid., p. 1362.

38. Harrison to Confidential Files, February 17, 1933, "Conversations," Harrison Papers.

39. Hoover to Roosevelt, February 18, 1933, President's Personal Files, File 820, Roosevelt Papers, Franklin D. Roosevelt Library. (Hereafter referred to as Roosevelt Papers.) Herbert Hoover, *The Memoirs of Herbert Hoover,* 3 vols. (New York, 1951-1952), III, pp. 203-204.

40. Roosevelt to Hoover, February 20, 1933, President's Personal Files, File 820, Roosevelt Papers, As a result of an oversight by Roosevelt's staff, this letter did not reach President Hoover until March 2, 1933. See covering letter of Roosevelt to Hoover, March 1, 1933, ibid.

41. Broadus Mitchell, *Depression Decade* (New York, 1947), p. 130.

2 The Crisis of March 1933

Saturday, March 4, 1933, dawned on a nation almost devoid of banking facilities. In the previous days and hours banking officials had worked feverishly to salvage the collapsing situation, but by Thursday, March 2, bank moratoria had been declared in twenty-one states. Day and night, conferences were held at the White House, the Treasury Department, the Federal Reserve Board, and at the offices of Federal Reserve banks around the country. Bankers and government officials sought a means to stem the floods of panic sweeping the nation. Plans were evolved, evaluated, and then discarded. Members of the new administration immediately began work upon arrival in Washington. Some of the old administration remained at their posts. All labored in unison to save the banks. For a time hope was held that the large banks in the financial centers would weather the storm; that with the inauguration of Franklin Roosevelt, a surge of confidence would sweep the country, the tide would turn, and conditions would be stabilized. Hope was in vain. No satisfactory solution was found, meetings disintegrated, the banking structure crumbled, and state by state the banks closed.

As bank holidays spread, and more and more states took action, Senator James Couzens, Republican from Michigan, proposed legislation to permit federal authorities to close national banks in those states in which other banks were already closed.[1] This was the only federal statutory measure enacted by Congress to meet the banking crisis. Remedial

banking legislation remained at an impasse. Representative
Steagall berated the Senate Banking and Currency Committee
for delaying action on his deposit guaranty plan.[2] Reports
circulated that last minute House action would be taken on
the Glass banking bill.[3] President Hoover, in a final plea to
Congress, urged its passage,[4] but no recommendation was
made by the president-elect. The bill remained in committee.

Hoover consulted with his legal advisers. Consideration
was given to the use of certain unrepealed presidential war
powers over bank withdrawals and foreign exchange. The
status of these powers, granted by the Trading with the
Enemy Act of 1917, was in doubt. Hoover's advisers felt
that "under another law, all war powers had been terminated
by the peace." The president conferred with Secretary of
the Treasury Mills and with Senator Glass, both of whom
held that "no certain power existed." On March 2, Hoover
requested the opinion of the Federal Reserve Board as to
the use of the emergency powers for the purpose of limiting
coin and currency withdrawals. He said: "If it is the view of
the Board that these powers should be exerted I would be
glad to have your recommendations, accompanied by a form
of proclamation as it would seem to me it should be issued
by me before banking hours tomorrow morning."[5]

That evening at a meeting of the Reserve Board, Eugene
Meyer reported that Attorney General William D. Mitchell
had authorized the board's counsel, Walter Wyatt, to tell the
secretary of the Treasury that there was "sufficient color of
authority" under the Trading with the Enemy Act to justify
presidential action. Later, that same night, while the board
was still in session, Secretary Mills qualified this statement,
advising the board that, while the attorney general "thought
that the President could act under the provisions of Section 5
of the Trading with the Enemy Act if he deemed the emergency great enough, the matter was not free from doubt."
Mills indicated that the attorney general "did not feel that

he should advise the President to do so without the consent and approval of the incoming Administration." The matter was discussed at length. The board concluded that the worsening conditions warranted the declaration of a banking holiday "for Friday, Saturday, and Monday, on the understanding that Congress would be called into special session not later than Tuesday, to enact appropriate legislation." This, it was felt, would bridge the administrations and would, of necessity, require the concurrence of the president-elect. Secretary Mills then contacted the newly designated Secretary of the Treasury, William Woodin, and advised him of the board's views.[6]

The Roosevelt forces were cognizant of the presidential powers granted under the Trading with the Enemy Act. The statute had been called to the attention of the president-elect by Rene Leon, a retired banker, who had served as adviser to the House Banking and Currency Committee. Leon suggested its use as a means of stopping some of the international banking houses from speculating in American gold. As a result of his conversation with Leon, Franklin Roosevelt sent Rexford Tugwell, a member of the Brain Trust, to Washington to check into the matter. Tugwell made cautious inquiries and was advised by Herbert Feis, economic adviser in the State Department, that the only copy of the act available at the Treasury Department was in the possession of Dan Bell, commissioner of Accounts and Deposits. Feis said that he had that copy on his desk and thought Tugwell "would be interested in looking at it." Tugwell went to Feis' office and found the particular clause that Roosevelt wanted to use "underlined in red." Tugwell felt this "obviously indicated that Ogden Mills and Mr. Hoover had taken a careful look at it." Tugwell next conferred with Democratic Senators Key Pittman of Nevada and James Byrnes of South Carolina and asked for their views. Neither senator was able to offer an opinion. In Tugwell's own opinion, "the interpretation depended on a semi-colon. That is to say, whether the entire paragraph of the Act had been repealed, or whether it had been repealed down to the semi-colon." Tugwell returned to Hyde Park and related the whole story to Roosevelt. He told the president-elect that he believed the required clause had not been repealed, but indicated he thought that Roosevelt "might get into trouble if he used it."[7]

On Friday, March 3, Franklin Roosevelt went to the White House for the traditional courtesy call on the outgoing president. When the social amenities were concluded, Hoover asked Secretary Mills and Governor Meyer of the Federal Reserve Board to join the meeting for a discussion of the banking situation. Roosevelt requested the attendance of Raymond Moley, his economic adviser. In the course of the discussion, Moley later related, President Hoover said he "felt a bank closing proclamation was unnecessary," that he believed "a proclamation controlling foreign exchange and withdrawals would be adequate." Hoover then pointed out that the issuance of such a proclamation would necessitate the use of emergency powers under the Trading with the Enemy Act. He felt it was extremely doubtful whether that act was still valid and indicated that his own attorney general was inclined to think not. If he issued such a proclamation, he feared the powers granted by the Trading with the Enemy Act might subsequently be disavowed by Congress. Hoover believed Roosevelt's assurance that Congress would not do this was indispensable. Without such assurance, the president said he could not proceed.[8]

Roosevelt declined to give such a guarantee. Reviewing the events of that hectic period in later years, Franklin Roosevelt justified his position:

> It is well to remember that during the trying days of January, February and the first three days of March, prior to my inauguration, I was a private citizen, wholly without authority, expressed or implied. . . . For me to have taken part in the daily relations

between the Executive and the Congress would have been, not only improper, but wholly useless.[9]

At the White House meeting, Roosevelt told Hoover that he had examined the act himself and had requested Senator Thomas Walsh, his own attorney general designate, for an opinion on the law. Before his untimely death on March 2, Walsh had reported that in an emergency he would rule "that the needed exercise of power was valid." Roosevelt then indicated that Homer Cummings, his new attorney general designate, was considering the question. For himself, Roosevelt stated he had "every reason to believe the requisite authority still existed." Declining to participate in joint action with the Hoover administration, upon leaving the White House Roosevelt turned to the president and said, "I shall be waiting at my hotel, Mr. President, to learn what you decide."[10]

That same afternoon Governor Meyer reported to the Federal Reserve Board and said that he felt the president would issue a proclamation declaring a bank holiday if the president-elect were to give his approval to such action. At 9:15 that night the board reconvened to take under consideration three drafts prepared by its own counsel—a draft of an executive order declaring a nationwide bank holiday; a draft of a joint resolution of Congress confirming the executive order if one should be issued; and a draft of a joint resolution of Congress declaring a nationwide bank holiday if that body wished to act. Since the Senate had adjourned for the day, the issuance of a presidential proclamation was the only course open. Meyer telephoned President Hoover to advise him of the board's deliberations. He informed him that the board felt that action was necessary that night. Since the president was still reluctant to act, the board determined to make a formal request urging the president to issue immediately a proclamation or executive order declaring a nationwide bank holiday. Secretary Mills and George James, members of the board who had not attended the meeting, were summoned so that the full board membership could participate.[11]

While those in attendance awaited the arrival of the absent members, word was received from the Federal Reserve banks in New York and Chicago. Eugene Stevens, chairman of the Federal Reserve Bank of Chicago, advised the Federal Reserve Board that the executive committee of the Chicago Bank had been in session with representatives of member banks. He transmitted to the board a resolution of the Chicago Bank's executive committee which called for the immediate declaration of a national bank holiday. Stevens emphasized that on the following day there would be "very large demands for gold "which would take practically all the gold the Chicago Reserve Bank held. He reported that "probably $100 million of Federal Reserve notes will be presented for redemption in gold," and that "one bank alone is asking $75 or $80 million dollars."[12]

From New York, George Harrison advised Secretary Mills and Governor Meyer that the New York Reserve Bank "could not pay out gold and currency much longer at the rate of the past few days." He put them on notice that one of three things should be done that night: a bank holiday should be declared; specie payments should be suspended; or reserve requirements should be suspended. However, Harrison thought the last alternative would be undesirable because "it would force the Federal Reserve to pay out further millions of dollars of gold and currency to hoarders." He believed the second alternative equally unattractive "since the suspension of specie payment might result in hysteria and panic," and would probably lead to a run on the country's banks. He concluded, therefore, that consideration should be given to the declaration of a national holiday. He felt this would permit "the country to calm down" and "would allow time

for the passage of legislation to remedy the situation." The
Federal Reserve Board in turn suggested that Governor
Herbert Lehman of New York be requested to declare a
holiday in his state. Harrison refused to make such a request
on behalf of the Federal Reserve Bank of New York since
he felt "a holiday in the State of New York might not relieve
the Federal Reserve Bank of New York, acting for the whole
System, of its obligation to pay out gold to foreigners." Moreover, he thought that it would be impossible for the country's
banking system to function properly if a holiday were declared
in New York. Such action, he believed, would cause great
confusion. He supported the declaration of a national holiday.[13]

In New York leading bankers gathered at the Federal
Reserve Bank to consider the banking crisis. George Harrison
reported to the Board of Directors of the New York Bank on
his conversation with the Federal Reserve Board. In the light
of his report, the directors advocated the immediate passage
of remedial legislation for the protection of the banking
situation. If that proved impossible, they supported the
declaration of a national bank holiday, and if a holiday could
not be declared, they felt gold payments should be suspended.
The views of the directors were transmitted to the Federal
Reserve Board, to Secretary of the Treasury Mills, and to
Secretary of the Treasury-designate Woodin. In reply, the
board reported to the New York Reserve Bank that "there is
practically no hope of remedial legislation being passed
tonight." Harrison, on behalf of the directors of the Federal
Reserve Bank of New York, then made a formal recommendation to the Federal Reserve Board that a national bank holiday
be declared.[14]

In Washington, the Federal Reserve Board, with its full
membership assembled, drafted its letter to President Hoover
recommending the proclamation of a national holiday. Extensive discussions took place between Secretary Mills and
other members of the board concerning the legality of such

a proclamation. While Mills supported the recommendation, he asked that a statement be inserted in the board's minutes indicating the doubtful status of the legislative base for such action. This was done, and at 12:30 A.M. Governor Meyer signed the letter which was dispatched by special messenger to the White House.[15]

Throughout the evening the president and the president-elect had conferred by phone. Both had kept in close touch with conditions around the country. Both had spoken to Governor Lehman of New York. No agreements were reached, and no statements were issued. Word was finally received at the Federal Reserve Board and at the Reserve Bank meetings that the president and president-elect had retired for the night and that there was no chance of a national bank holiday being declared. Meanwhile, at the Treasury Department members of the secretary's staff were joined by members of the Roosevelt entourage. The staff had reviewed the bank figures for the day. It was clear that the banks would have to be protected against runs. They telephoned the governors of all the states that had not already suspended banking operations to induce them to agree to the declaration of a brief holiday. All were contacted except Governor Henry Horner of Illinois. Only one, Governor Herbert Lehman of New York, was reluctant to act.[16]

In New York the all-night session at the Federal Reserve Bank continued. Discussion turned to the declaration of a state holiday. George Harrison phoned Governor Lehman at his Park Avenue home where state banking authorities had gathered. They discussed the declaration of a state holiday. Lehman told Harrison that earlier in the day, at the instigation of the New York Clearing House banks, he had made a statement to the effect that he would not declare a holiday. He indicated that the Clearing House bankers had stated that "they would cooperate if he wanted to declare a bank holiday, but they would not request him to do so." Lehman felt they were not cooperating. He told Harrison that he wished to serve notice on the Clearing House bankers and on the Federal Reserve Bank of New York that "if anything goes wrong" he would state publically that "the Clearing House bankers and Mr. Harrison [had] been asked to confer" with him and had refused. Harrison informed the governor that he was willing to confer immediately. After further consideration, however, it was decided that Harrison should remain at the Reserve Bank where he could keep in touch with the governor, the Reserve Board, and the situation in Washington.[17]

At the Reserve Bank discussions of the banking situation continued. George Davison, president of the Central Hanover Bank of New York, took issue with Governor Lehman's views. He felt that a holiday in New York should not be pinned on either the Clearing House banks or the Federal Reserve Bank. He observed that if the governor consulted his superintendent of banks, the superintendent's recommendation should be sufficient backing for the governor's action. It was George Harrison's view that the Federal Reserve Bank of New York alone should not be put in the position of requesting a holiday. He said, "at most we should join with the Superintendent of Banks and the Clearing House banks in requesting such a holiday." Davison pointed out that the prestige of the Clearing House banks would be damaged if they appeared to be seeking a bank holiday. He thought that the banks would like to have a holiday declared because it would prevent further bank failures and would save the gold supply. He reported, however, "all but one of the banks had agreed, that they would rather stay open and take their beating, then ask for a holiday." After further discussion the position of the Clearing House banks with respect to the declaration of a state holiday was transmitted to the board in Washington.[18] In a short time, after receiving word from Washington that there was no possibility of a national bank holiday, Harrison left the meeting in progress at the Federal Reserve Bank and joined the conference at Governor Lehman's home. Shortly thereafter, he telephoned the directors meeting at the New York Reserve Bank and asked for authority to request a holiday in the state of New York. He said that "the Clearing House banks and the Superintendent of Banks would join the request."[19]

In Washington, at the Federal Reserve Board, no further word was received from the White House. At 2:22 that morning, Secretary Mills reported he had received information that, in all probability, the governors of Illinois and New York would declare holidays in their respective states. Less than an hour later, Chairman Stevens of the Federal Reserve Bank of Chicago advised the board that a proclamation was being drafted by the governor of Illinois, and at 3:10 A.M. Harrison reported that a legal holiday would be declared by the governor of New York. At 3:00 A.M. Governor Horner issued a proclamation closing the banks of Illinois, and at 4:20 A.M. Governor Lehman proclaimed a two-day holiday in New York.[20]

So it was that on March 4 the nation awoke to a state of bank paralysis. The banks in the financial centers of the country remained closed. By late afternoon all forty-eight states had declared holidays. That morning the Seventy-second Congress met to conclude its final business. Upon the adjournment of the old Congress, the new Senate immediately convened in special session. The oath of office was administered to John Nance Garner, the new vice-president, and at 1:08 P.M. Franklin Delano Roosevelt was inaugurated as president of the United States. Then in a firm and ringing voice, he spoke to a nation tense with anxiety. He offered leadership and asked for the people's support. He indicted the bankers, denouncing them as "the money changers" who "have fled from their high seats in the temple of our civilization." He demanded safeguards "against a return of the evils of the old order." He proclaimed that "there must be strict supervision of all banking and credits and investments; there must be an end to speculation with other people's money, and there must be provision for an adequate sound currency." The new president sought the assistance of the new Congress and of the states. He promised action and warned that he would, if necessary, ask the Congress for "broad executive power to wage a war against the emergency, as great as the power that would be given to me, if we were in fact invaded by a foreign foe." He concluded on a note of hope, and asked for God's guidance in the days to come.[21]

At the conclusion of the inauguration ceremony, members of the Senate returned to their chamber and quickly approved Roosevelt's cabinet appointments. Later that same day, in an unprecedented ceremony at the White House, the entire cabinet was sworn into office. Throughout the day meetings were held at the Treasury Department and at the Federal Reserve Board. Word went out to leading bankers to convene in Washington the following day. That night the president conferred with Secretary Woodin and Attorney General Cummings. Woodin promised to have emergency legislation ready by Thursday, March 9.

On Sunday, March 5, the first meeting of the cabinet was held. Secretary Woodin, after a morning of conferences with bankers hastily summoned from across the country, reported that the bankers had no plan of their own to solve the national emergency. Cabinet discussion centered on the use of the emergency powers under Section 5 of the Trading with the Enemy Act. Attorney General Cummings was consulted and indicated that he would give his official assent to the use of the emergency powers.[22] Work began on the preparation of a proclamation declaring a national bank holiday. That evening the president issued his first procla-

mation. He summoned the Congress to convene in extraordinary session on Thursday, March 9, the day on which
Secretary Woodin had agreed to have ready emergency
banking legislation.[23] At 1:00 A.M. Monday morning, March 6,
a second proclamation was issued. It was based on the drafts
previously prepared at the Treasury Department and at the
Federal Reserve Board for the use of President Hoover.
Using this proclamation, Franklin Roosevelt ordered a bank
holiday to extend from Monday, March 6, through Thursday,
March 9, "to be observed and maintained by all banking
institutions and all branches thereof in the United States of
America, including Territories and insular possessions,"
during which time "all banking transactions shall be
suspended."[24]

Meanwhile, at the Treasury Department, Republicans and
Democrats, bankers and banking authorities, congressional
leaders, and members of the administration met to work out
a plan to restore confidence in the banks and provide for
their reopening. Meetings began on Sunday morning and
continued around the clock. Consideration was given to the
adoption of some form of government guarantee for bank
deposits. The discussions continued into the afternoon but
no conclusions were reached. Finally, after consultation
with President Roosevelt, Secretary Woodin appointed a
subcommittee under the chairmanship of George W. Davison
of the Central Hanover Bank of New York. The subcommittee continued to explore the possibility of government
guarantees. Two plans evolved, one of which called for a flat
5 percent guarantee of unfrozen bank assets, and the other
which proposed a sliding scale guarantee based on individual
assets in individual banks. Work continued into the night.
The next morning the subcommittee again met. Secretary
Woodin was informed of developments. That afternoon, the
subcommittee reported to the general committee and recommended that banks be allowed to reopen "under a govern-

ment guarantee of 100%, 75%, 50%, and 25% as the condition of the Bank would warrant."[25]

Prior to the summons to Washington most of the bankers had been in constant conference in their own cities and states. Nerves had now reached the breaking point. Disagreements and arguments abounded. There was no unity of thought on purposes or methods. It soon became obvious that no progress would be made. That afternoon Governor Harrison told Secretary Woodin that he "did not think they would get anywhere," that, as he saw it, "he [Woodin] and the President, in the light of the various views expressed, would have to make up their minds what they wanted to do." Woodin went to the White House to consult with the president. The new administration did not favor a government guarantee. That night, a general meeting was held at the Treasury Department. Woodin thanked the bankers for their discussions, but said "that he and the President and his advisers would have to decide upon a policy." Without formally dismissing the subcommittee, he told them there was no occasion for them to continue their work.[26]

The meeting broke up, but a small group[27] remained behind and endeavored to work out a plan that would not involve a government guarantee, but would permit "the immediate opening of the good sound banks, speedy reorganization of those not 100% [sound] and the eventual liquidation of those that could not reopen." The difficulty lay in the gap between the opening of the good banks and the reorganization of the Class B banks, or those not 100 percent. Without finding a solution, the meeting finally adjourned. Later that night Governor Harrison became convinced "that the only thing to do was to give the reserve banks the authority to make loans to individuals, corporations and others, against [their holdings in] government securities." This, he felt, "would do more than anything else to fill the gap since it allowed all owners of government bonds, wherever located, and whether or not they had bank contacts, to go to the reserve banks with their bonds, borrow on their 90 day notes and get currency." The next morning, when he arrived at the Treasury Department, he consulted with Davison, former Secretary Mills, and former Under Secretary Arthur Ballantine. All saw merit in his plan.[28]

On Monday night, after the general meeting adjourned, Secretary Woodin and Raymond Moley conferred, seeking a comprehensive formula to solve the banking crisis. They concluded "that every step taken must be tested less on the basis of its ultimate desirability from a financial point of view than on the basis of its immediate effect in restoring confidence." Recognizing the "need for swift and staccato action," they determined conditions warranted the opening of as many banks as could be opened within the realm of safety since they felt "the greater number opened, the greater the probability of confidence in banks generally." They recognized that "conventional banking methods" should be stressed and that the "so called left-wing presidential advisers" should be blacked out during the emergency.[29]

Across the country, as deliberations in Washington proceeded, state legislatures met in emergency sessions to cope with local problems resulting from the bank holiday. In many states governors were granted extraordinary powers, and debt moratoria were declared. The shortage of currency was acute in communities both large and small. In some localities payrolls were met by cash payment, but in many places the use of scrip was authorized to meet payrolls and provide for the continuation of local business. Clearing houses, local bankers, and banking authorities cooperated in developing plans for the issuance of scrip. An Associated Press release reported that "financial associations in several states had printing presses humming to the tune of millions in scrip."[30] New York bankers urged the adoption on a national basis of a plan to use clearing house certificates in place of checks during the emergency.[31] By Monday night, the scrip idea had gained so much favor that the conferees meeting in Washington took it for granted that it would be carried through.[32] Treasury officials from the Hoover administration advised against it. There were protests that it would discriminate against nonmember clearing house banks. On Tuesday morning, Secretary Woodin decided against it. He said to Raymond Moley:

> We don't have to issue scrip! We don't need it. These bankers have hypnotized themselves and us. We can issue currency against the sound assets of the banks. The Federal Reserve Act lets us print all we'll need. And it won't frighten the people. It won't look like stage money. It'll be money that looks like real money.[33]

Woodin and Moley went to the White House, talked with the president, and received his approval of their general plan. Woodin then went to the Treasury Department where he called together Harrison, Davison, Mills, and Ballantine. He outlined to them a plan "which opened all good banks, that is 100% banks, and then [what he called B banks] that is those that might ultimately be reorganized on a sound basis." He then said to "hold onto your chairs and look out for my ceiling" and proposed "a plan which called for the immediate conversion of all government bonds—the full $21 billion into cash at par." This was apparently the president's own plan. Both Harrison and Mills voiced vigorous objections, Mills deeming "it was destruction and an impossible thing to contemplate converting all of the government time obligations into a demand liability payable in cash at 100%," and Harrison declaring "that it was ruinous in itself, and would invite convertibility of all other government obligations, such as the liability to veterans, into cash at once." Woodin implied that the president was set on this plan and that they would have to give him some good alternatives. Davison stated that

George Harrison "had a suggestion which might satisfy the President."[34]

Governor Harrison then outlined the plan he had discussed earlier that morning. He said that if the Reserve banks were given the authority to make loans to owners of government bonds, they would have "a very strong arm control," through the exercise of rate pressure upon the borrowers, to bring about the liquidation of the 90-day notes. This, he believed, would hold down currency inflation. In the absence of a government guarantee, Harrison suggested that only sound banks be opened and sufficient currency made available to enable them to pay off all deposits in full. He believed that the present situation afforded the best opportunity to effect "a final cleanup of the banking position by opening (1) the good banks, (2) reorganizing those which have a possibility of reorganizing, and (3) liquidating those that were hopeless." Harrison said that this program involved "a very definite affirmative currency program, showing to the country that there is plenty available." It would, however, necessitate enlarging the powers of the Reserve banks to do three things:

> (1) make loans to any member bank that is open on the basis of its sound assets to pay off its deposits; (2) to enable us to issue Federal reserve bank notes not only against any governments we might own or acquire, but also against these sound member bank assets; (3) to include in the eligible collateral for Federal reserve bank notes the obligations of individuals, firms or corporations secured by government bonds.[35]

When Harrison concluded outlining his plan, Woodin requested that he "put the program on paper in order that he [Woodin] might take it to the President." Harrison complied. With the aid of Ogden Mills and George Davison he drafted a memorandum which Woodin read with apparent satisfaction. Meyer of the Federal Reserve Board was called in, presented with the program, and agreed to the plan. Then Woodin, accompanied by Davison and Ballantine, went to the White House to present the plan to the president. Later in the afternoon Woodin returned and said "the President had agreed to the program in its entirety and that [they] should proceed to draft the necessary legislation."[36]

The same group met that evening at 9:30, together with members of the staff of the Federal Reserve Board. Ballantine read the program to them, answered some questions, and told them to get to work. An all-night session followed. The next morning they hammered out the draft of a bill. This was revised by Harrison, Ballantine, Wyatt (counsel to the Federal Reserve Board), and a Mr. Woods of the Legislative Drafting Bureau of the Congress. That afternoon a final draft was sent to the White House. At the White House every paragraph was read, there was constant checking back with those at the Treasury Department, and necessary changes were made. Congressional leaders then were called to confer with the president. By 2:00 A.M. on the morning of March 9, the bill was ready for Congress.[37]

At noon on March 9, Congress convened. At 3:00 P.M. a message from the president was read to the House and to the Senate. The president said that "our first task is to open all sound banks." To accomplish this he asked for "the immediate enactment of legislation, giving to the executive branch of the government control over banks, for the protection of depositors." He requested "authority to open such banks as have already been ascertained to be in sound condition, and other such banks as may be found to require reorganization to put them on a sound basis." In addition, he required amendments to the Federal Reserve Act "to provide for such additional currency to meet all demands without increasing the unsecured indebtedness of the Government of the United States." The president urged immediate action, and stressed that "a continuation of the strangulation of banking facilities is unthinkable."[38]

An hour later, the Emergency Banking Act, which only
the congressional leaders had seen, was read, briefly debated, and passed by the House of Representatives. Republican Representative Bertrand Snell voiced the views of fellow
Congressmen when he said: "The house is burning down,
and the President of the United States says this is the way to
put out the fire. And to me, at this time, there is only one
answer to the question, that is to give the President what he
says is necessary to meet the situation."[39]

The bill then went to the Senate where Huey Long
attempted to amend it so that the president would have the
power to draw all state banks into the Federal Reserve
System. This brief debate was cut off when Carter Glass
declared:

> There are provisions in the bill to which in ordinary times I would
> not dream of subscribing, but we have a situation that invites the
> patriotic cooperation and aid of every man who has any regard
> for his country and for its business interest. I appeal to you Senators,
> not to load it down with amendments. Let us accept the bill, almost
> if not unanimously passed by the House of Representatives, and
> not alter it and have to go into controversial conference that might
> take us beyond the time when aid is imperatively needed.[40]

By 7:00 P.M. the bill passed the Senate by a vote of 73 to 7.
It was sent to the White House and two hours later Roosevelt
signed it into law. The tasks that remained were to reopen
the banks, restore the people's confidence, and begin the
rebuilding of the banking system.

That night the president issued a proclamation which
extended the bank holiday to allow time for the Treasury
and Federal Reserve officials to reopen the banks. On
Friday the job of checking hundreds upon hundreds of bank
reports began. On Saturday the president issued a statement
to the press in which he said that banks would be opened

progressively on Monday, Tuesday, and Wednesday of the following week. Member banks in the Federal Reserve cities were to open on Monday morning.[41]

On Sunday night, March 12, the president spoke to the nation by radio. He reviewed what had been done over the past few days, why it was done, and what the next steps would be. He explained why all banks would not open simultaneously. He said: "It is necessary that the reopening of banks be extended over a period in order to permit the banks to make application for necessary loans, to obtain currency to meet their requirements and to enable the government to make common-sense check-ups." In response to a flood of telegrams received from the governors of the various states, the president promised that state banks, not members of the Federal Reserve System, "can and will receive assistance from member banks and from the Reconstruction Finance Corporation." He asked for the cooperation of the public and "its intelligent support and use of a reliable system." He said:

> We had a bad banking situation. Some of our bankers had shown themselves either incompetent or dishonest in their handling of the people's funds. They had used the money entrusted to them in speculation and unwise loans. This was of course not true in the vast majority of our banks, but it was true in enough of them to shock the people for a time into a sense of insecurity and to put them into a frame of mind where they did not differentiate, but seemed to assume that the acts of a comparative few had tainted them all. It was the Government's job to straighten out this situation and to do it as quickly as possible—and the job is being performed.[42]

The next morning, Monday, March 13, the banks in the Reserve cities reopened. Banks in other cities were opened according to plan. The public began redepositing its money and the wheels of the banking industry again turned. The emergency had caught the bankers of the nation in the

vortex of disaster. The cumulative impact of local banking crises and public alarm made it imperative that the
federal government take the lead in restoring public confidence in the American banking system. On the local level,
in many instances, bankers made substantial contributions
in devising ways to cope with local problems. The banking
disaster could not be contained as panic and fear increased.
The failure of the banking community to offer an acceptable
and comprehensive plan of action when it was called to
Washington to aid the government was symptomatic of the
ills that beset the American banking system. Lack of unity,
devotion to local interests, and failure to comprehend the
overall banking problems of the nation were deeply embedded
in the dual banking concept.

As the crisis passed and the Emergency Banking Act went
into effect, the American banking community rallied in
behalf of the administration's program. They had praise for
Franklin Roosevelt and supported in full the steps he had taken.

NOTES

1. *Congressional Record,* LXXVI, p. 4460.

2. Ibid., p. 5363.

3. *The New York Times,* February 20, 1933.

4. *Congressional Record,* LXXVI, p. 4504.

5. Herbert Hoover, *The Memoirs of Herbert Hoover,* 3 vols. (New York:
1951-1952), III, pp. 208-211.

6. Charles S. Hamlin, MS Diary, March 2, 1933, Charles S. Hamlin Family
Papers, Library of Congress. (Hereafter referred to as "Hamlin Diary.")

7. Rexford G. Tugwell, "The Reminiscences of Rexford G. Tugwell,"
36-19 Oral History Collection, Butler Library, Columbia University. (Hereafter
referred to as Tugwell, "Reminiscences.")

8. Raymond Moley, *After Seven Years* (New York, 1939), p. 146.

9. S. I. Rosenman, ed., *The Public Papers and Addresses of Franklin D.
Roosevelt,* 13 vols. (New York, 1938-1950), I, p. 869.

10. Moley, *After Seven Years,* p. 146.

11. "Hamlin Diary," March 3, 1933.

12. Ibid.

13. Federal Reserve Bank of New York, Board of Directors, Special Meeting, March 3, 1933, "Discussion Notes," Harrison Papers.

14. Ibid.

15. "Hamlin Diary," March 4, 1933.

16. Moley, *After Seven Years*, p. 147.

17. Federal Reserve Bank of New York, Board of Directors, Special Meeting, March 3, 1933, "Discussion Notes," Harrison Papers.

18. Ibid.

19. Ibid.

20. "Hamlin Diary," March 4, 1933.

21. *Congressional Record*, LXXVII, pp. 5-6.

22. Franklin D. Roosevelt, *On Our Way* (New York, 1934), pp. 4-5.

23. *Congressional Record*, LXXVII, p. 41.

24. [U.S. Treasury Department] , *Documents and Statements Pertaining to the Banking Emergency*, 2 vols. (Washington, D.C., 1933), I, pp. 1-2.

25. Harrison to Confidential Files, March 12, 1933, "Conversations," Harrison Papers.

26. Ibid.

27. This group consisted of Ogden Mills, George Davison, Adolph Berle, F. Floyd Awalt, A. Goldenweiser, and George Harrison. Ibid.

28. Ibid.

29. Moley, *After Seven Years*, pp. 150-151.

30. *The New York Times*, March 6, 1933.

31. Ibid., March 7, 1933.

32. Harrison to Confidential Files, March 12, 1933. "Conversations," Harrison Papers.

33. Moley, *After Seven Years*, p. 51.

34. Harrison to Confidential Files, March 12, 1933, "Conversations," Harrison Papers.

35. Ibid.

36. Ibid.

37. Ibid.

38. *Congressional Record*, LXXVII, pp. 45, 75-76.

39. Ibid., p. 76.

40. Ibid., p. 58.

41. [U.S. Treasury Department] , *Documents and Statements Pertaining to the Banking Emergency*, I, p. 7.

42. Ibid., pp. 9-11.

Table 6.
Branch Banking in the United States, 1900-1935

Year	National Banks With Branches	State Banks With Branches	Total Banks With Branches	Total Number of Branches	National Bank Branches	State Bank Branches
1900	5	82	87	119	5	114
1905	5	191	196	350	5	345
1910	9	283	292	548	12	536
1915	12	385	397	785	26	759
1920	21	509	530	1,281	63	1,218
1925	130	590	720	2,525	318	2,207
1930	166	585	751	3,522	1,042	2,480
1935	181	636	817	3,155	1,329	1,826

SOURCE: *Historical Statistics of the United States: Colonial Times to 1957* (Washington, D.C.: Department of Commerce, 1960), p. 635.

3 The Bankers' Views on Bank Reform

Prior to the crisis of March 1933, the banking community challenged the need for overall bank reform legislation. All bankers did not unite in total opposition to the Glass banking bill, but few accepted, without reservation, the entire omnibus measure. Major controversy centered on five proposals: (1) extension of branch banking by national banks, (2) limitations on the use of Federal Reserve credit for speculative purposes, (3) separation of commercial from investment banking, (4) divorcement of national banks from their security affiliates, and (5) more rigid control over all banks within the national and Federal Reserve banking systems. These, together with the Steagall deposit guarantee plan, were widely debated in banking journals, before congressional committees, and by bankers' associations throughout the country. Over and above these specific issues loomed the fear that the federal government would seek to bring all banking regulations within its orbit through the nationalization of the banking system, an issue which created additional division and dissension within the banking fraternity.

The problem of branch banking predated the depression. In the first three decades of the twentieth century, the number of banking institutions maintaining branches had increased from 87 to 751, and the number of branches established had risen from 119 to 3,522 (see Table 6). This increase marked a departure from unit banking practices and

caused a concern which was intensified by the overall consolidation and merger movement of the 1920s. Throughout
the nation the growth of branch banking had not been
uniform. Because under the dual banking system supervision of banks was divided between the federal and state
banking authorities, branching statutes differed from state
to state. Some states permitted statewide branch banking,
other states allowed limited branch banking, while still
others expressly prohibited the establishment of branches.
A few states had no statutory enactments whatsoever on
branch banking.

Within the limitations of the federal banking laws, branch
banking for federally supervised banks was considerably
influenced by state statutory provisions. Banks subject to
federal regulation fell into two categories: national banks
and Federal Reserve member banks. Although the National
Bank Act did not expressly prohibit the establishment of
branches, the law had been so interpreted since its passage
in 1863. Nevertheless, some national banks did maintain
branches. This resulted when state banks with previously
established branches merged with or converted to national
banks. In such cases these institutions were permitted to
retain their established branches. The Federal Reserve Act,
enacted in 1913, made no provision for branch banking.
National banks, which were required to join the Federal
Reserve System, continued to be governed by the provisions of the National Bank Act. State banks electing to
join the Federal Reserve System were initially governed by
the provisions of the banking laws of the individual states,
but in 1916, by policy decision, and in 1924, by formal
regulation, the Federal Reserve Board required state member
banks to obtain board approval before establishing additional
branches. This narrowed to some extent the inequities that
existed between state member banks and national banks.
The disparity between the two was further redressed when in

1921 the comptroller of the Currency ruled that national banks could establish limited service offices for the purpose of receiving deposits and checks. In 1923 his ruling was upheld by the attorney general, but in 1924, a halt was called to further liberalization of branch banking for national banks when the Supreme Court ruled that under the National Bank Act no more than one full service office could be maintained by a national bank. By 1925, within the limitations established by statutory regulation and judicial interpretation, 130 national banks maintained a combined total of 318 branches as compared to a combined total of 2,207 branches established by 590 state banks (see Table 6).

As branch banking continued to spread, there was increased concern with respect to the provisions of both state and federal laws. In the United States, single-office unit banks predominated. Such institutions feared the growth of branch banking and pressed for restrictive branching laws. As a result, a number of states enacted laws to prohibit branch banking. Nevertheless, wherever permitted by law, branch banking continued to increase and the restrictive features of federal law moved federal banking authorities to advocate a more liberal branch bank policy. In 1927 this resulted in the enactment of the McFadden Act. Under this law state banks which were members of the Federal Reserve System, or which subsequently became members of the Federal Reserve System under their own charters or by conversion into national banks, were permitted to legally retain all branches established prior to the date of approval of the act, regardless of location of the branch. They were forbidden, however, to establish new branches outside the corporate limits of their head office cities. National banks were authorized to retain branches established prior to the date of enactment, and to establish new branches within the limits of the city, town, or village in which they were situated if such establishment of operations was at the time permitted to state banks by the laws of the state in question.[1]

The controversy over branch banking did not abate with the enactment of new federal and state branch banking laws. Almost immediately following the enactment of the McFadden Act, Comptroller of the Currency John W. Pole urged the institution of trade area branch banking for national banks. Under this plan, national banks would be permitted to establish branches in an area related to the economic needs of a given territory, and would not be restricted to the geographic boundaries of the individual states. In 1930 the comptroller repeated his recommendation when, in view of the large number of bank failures, he held that trade area branch banking "would bring the benefits and protection of the strong well managed banks to the rural area where so many failures had taken place."[2] Secretary of the Treasury Ogden Mills supported trade area branch banking. In his annual report for 1931, he stated that "such a step would afford better management, service and diversification with a greater measure of safety than can now be obtained under our present system."[3] Growing concern over the number of bank failures, the continued existence of statutory inequities for federally supervised banks, and the spread of chain banking systems, which through the holding company device were able to circumvent restrictive federal branch banking laws, led inevitably to consideration of branch banking by Congress.

From 1930 to 1933 the battle over branch banking raged. Bankers appeared before congressional committees to offer testimony for and against changes in the branch banking provisions of federal law. Some bankers went beyond the recommendations of the comptroller of the Currency and advocated nationwide branch banking. A. P. Giannini, founder of California's Bank of America, the nation's leading branch banking institution, was the foremost supporter of such a step. In 1930 he told the House Banking and Currency Committee: "There is only one way to do banking, and that is on a branch basis, with one capitalization, one charter, and one responsibility." He called for "nation wide and world wide branch banking," stating: "It is coming gentlemen and you cannot stop it, and you are bucking up against a stone wall if you try. You cannot buck natural economic forces."[4] Others supported this position. In 1932 Edward Ball of the Atlantic National Bank of Jacksonville, Florida, testified before a Senate hearing that "we believe branch banking would be a good thing either within the State or throughout the United States."[5]

While only a few bankers supported nationwide branch banking, a greater number accepted the position of the comptroller of the Currency calling for trade area branch banking which would permit the extension of national bank operations beyond state boundaries. Henry M. Robinson, chairman of the board of the Security-First National Bank of Los Angeles and an adviser to President Hoover, favored the comptroller's recommendation. In 1931 Robinson told the Glass subcommittee that trade area branch banking would offer better control than group or chain banking. He based his conclusions on the experience of his own institution where both methods had been tried. He stressed the fact that growth should be gradual and that the number of branches allowed should be regulated in proportion to the capital of the bank.[6] Other bankers opposed this viewpoint. Charles F. Zimmerman, president of the First National Bank of Huntington, Pennsylvania, testified that:

> I am simply astonished to think that Congress would seriously consider the proposal to grant the right for a national bank to cross State lines in so-called trade areas. I am at a loss to know where any substantial demands of that sort should arise so far as the practical administration of banking is concerned, and so far as the service of banking to its constituency is concerned.[7]

Although many bankers recognized the inequities of the
branch banking laws with respect to federally supervised
banks, they feared that in remedying this situation an adverse
imbalance might result for state banks. Rudolph Hecht,
president of the Hibernia Bank and Trust Company of New
Orleans, shared this fear:

> I have fought many times, and I am prepared to fight now, against
> any discrimination that would make it difficult for a national
> bank to compete properly with a State bank. I am in favor per-
> sonally . . . of the extension of branch banking on a state-wide
> basis. Where the State banks are permitted to do it, I believe there
> should be an equality of opportunity for the two systems on a
> sound basis.[8]

Others opposed this position. Thomas Preston, president
of the Hamilton National Bank of Chattanooga, Tennessee,
believed branch banking should not be limited to the provisions of state laws. He told the Senate subcommittee: "You
gentlemen would follow the Tennessee Legislature and it
looks to me like it would be fairer for the Tennessee Legislature to follow Congress." He emphasized that equating the
operations of national banks with those of state banks would
result in "some national banks in some States" having "a
state-wide basis, while in Tennessee, they would not have it."[9]

Spokesmen for the large banks engaged in an extensive
correspondent banking business did not favor widespread
liberalization of the branch bank policy. George W. Davison,
president of the Central Hanover Bank and Trust Company
of New York City, claimed that the correspondent bank
system was "very much better than branch banking, in that,
in each community you have a responsible body or bank
that knows the needs of the community." He believed that
the extension of branch banking would simply "use the
remote community as a source of contributing, in a sense,
simply draining money out of that community to the money

centers."[10] Davison's views were shared by Albert H. Wiggin, spokesman for the Chase National Bank of New York City. Wiggin told the Senate subcommittee that "every community in this country that will support a bank is well cared for already." He indicated that Chase had a very long experience in acting as correspondent, and that "we do not know of a case where a solvent bank has been permitted to fail from lack of accommodation from its correspondent."[11] Wiggin did not believe that branch banking would strengthen the banking system.

Despite the spread of branch banking, the vast majority of banks in the United States were single-office unit banks. The unit bankers voiced the strongest objections to the extension of branch banking. They feared the competition that would result if large banking organizations were permitted to extend their operations, and held that local communities were best served by local banks. By sheer numerical strength, the unit bankers were in a position to bring pressure on their state legislatures and Congress. They dominated the state bankers associations, and made it impossible for the American Bankers Association to take more than an equivocal position on the subject of branch banking. Typical of the attitude of the unit banker was that expressed by Don Devey of the Farmers State Bank of Westport, South Dakota:

> The provisions in the Glass bill restricting branch banking to those states that permit State branch banking should be sustained. There is going to be a fight on this restriction—the branch, chain and group banking interests in the country are going to bring their influence to bear against this restriction in the hope that it will provide another wedge into the dream of national branch banking over the entire country.[12]

Many bankers throughout the country were opposed to any expansion of branch banking. In the summer of 1932, the

Association of Independent Unit Banks was organized.[13]
In January 1933, this association issued a statement calling
for the defeat of the branch banking provision of the Glass
banking bill.[14] State bankers associations fought vigorously
against the provision. Unit bankers were urged to combat
the measure. Journals of bankers associations carried the
fight to their membership. *The Texas Bankers Record,* one
such publication, stated editorially:

> At Washington the situation has greater and darker possibilities.
> There is sure to be a "1933 Banking Law." . . . It will more than
> probably contain section 19 of the Glass Bill, or similar provisions
> providing for state-wide branch banking. This is not to discourage
> you, but to stir you to the point of making your opposition to
> these proposals known, and for you to prime your guns and fire
> when you see the whites of the enemy's eyes.[15]

Throughout this period the National Association of Supervisors of State Banks fought against the proposal to liberalize
the branch bank provisions of the National Bank Act. As early
as 1930, M. E. Bristow, president of the Association, stated to
the membership: "Frankly gentlemen of the Convention, I do
not think Congress can justify its action if it attempts to force
branch banking on any state against its will. . . . The only
justification for Congress to act in the matter is to give national
banks the same rights to branching as their state competitors
have."[16] In 1931, his successor, S. A. Adams, Iowa State
superintendent of banks, reviewed federal proposals and said:
"It is preposterous to think that this country will ever adopt
any measure which will even hamper, let alone do away with
the state bank system. . . . We simply demand that the two
great systems of banking in this country continue on an
equal basis, and it should not be necessary to make a fight
for this principle."[17] In 1932, J. S. Love, superintendent of
banks for Mississippi, reiterated these thoughts, and stated
that the branch bank section of the Glass bill was the most

objectionable part of the bill since it tended "to do away with the independent unit banking system."[18]

In the early 1930s, as Congress considered bank reform legislation, branch banking was one of the most controversial issues debated. Those who opposed it feared a concentration of power, unfair competition, and a decline of local interest in banking. Ultimately, they saw in it the death of the dual banking system in the United States. Those who supported the extension of branch banking believed it would result in better service to banking customers. Eventually, they felt that weak banks would be eliminated and that the banking structure of the nation would be strengthened. As economic conditions worsened and banking problems grew more acute, interest shifted from the branch bank controversy to issues of more immediate concern. Only the momentum of the first hundred days of the Roosevelt administration would enable the proponents of branch banking to achieve a measure of success in liberalizing the branch banking provisions of federal law.

Although the branch banking controversy predated the depression, it was the stock market crash of 1929 that gave rise to the concern for more rigid control over bank activities in the field of securities operations. In February 1929 the Federal Reserve Board had taken note of the substantial increase in brokers' loans made by member banks, and had warned that "the use of Federal Reserve credit for speculative loans is not in harmony with the intent of the Federal reserve act, nor is it conducive to the wholesome operations of the banking and credit systems."[19] Nevertheless, throughout the year, brokers' loans continued to grow in volume; when the stock market broke in October, attention focused on the alarming extent to which the country's credit had been committed to securities speculation. All credit channeled into the stock market frenzy did not come under Federal Reserve control. A substantial amount of money was funneled into stock market speculation through non-bank lenders. Even so, the Federal Reserve System and member bank activities became prime targets for investigations that emphasized the dangers of securities operations as an adjunct to banking. Serious questions were also raised with respect to bank subsidiaries and affiliated security companies. As investigations proceeded, widespread publicity was given to those cases of mismanagement and malfeasances that were uncovered. In the general outcry that resulted all bankers were condemned. The inference was that bank funds had been manipulated and bank assets had been channeled into securities speculation. Particular emphasis was placed on the elaborate financial relationships that had been constructed so that existing laws could be circumvented. Although much that was done was not illegal, the implications shocked the public and spurred congressional action to bring under control the speculative activities of those banks that came within the scope of federal regulation. A prime motivating force behind the Senate banking investigation was the desire of Senator Glass to tighten the provisions of the Federal Reserve Act so that Federal Reserve funds could not be used for speculative purposes. He proposed to do this by drastically limiting security loans and the security holdings of member banks, and by directing the Federal Reserve Board to use all its authority to discourage such operations by commercial banks.

These proposals, incorporated in the Glass banking bill, met with considerable resistance from members of the banking community. Recognizing the pitfalls that existed in the banking system, bankers held that control could be achieved by self-regulation rather than by new legislation. In 1931 Henry T. Ferriss, president of the Investment Bankers Association, stated that "we, the investment bankers, as well as the commercial bankers and other credit agencies have it within our power to minimize the ultimate evils of periods of inflation by discouraging the granting of credit based on values resulting from rapid price increases."[20] In 1932 Allan M. Pope of the First of Boston Corporation told the members of the Investment Bankers Association that "You cannot legislate speculation out of existence—you can in some instances minimize its effect." He took issue with the proposed legislative measures:

> In practically all instances they fail to reach the fundamental wrong, a wrong which since the war crept into the conduct of our business, and which is today being steadily corrected from within our ranks to the benefit of the small investor and of the large, and hence to the benefit of ourselves. This wrong cannot be legislated out of existence. We alone control the power to correct it.[21]

Most bankers who came before the Senate Banking and Currency Subcommittee opposed an increase in Federal Reserve powers over member bank lending policies. W. R. McQuaid, president of the Barnett National Bank of Jacksonville, Florida, asked, "How can the Board determine for me and 7,000 other banks what our particular local needs are, irrespective of any speculative conditions?" McQuaid believed that legislation should not "so closely define what a bank should and should not do, as to let that entirely take the place of management and judgement in the operation of a bank."[22] Some bankers, however, did support the extension of federal control over the speculative activities of member banks. Charles Zimmerman (president of the First National Bank in Huntington, Pennsylvania), who had denounced the branch banking provision of the Glass bill, now came to the defense of the measure:

> I am numbered among those who believe that for the good of banking in this country it is entirely right and proper that more authority be lodged in the Federal Reserve Board than heretofore.

I am entirely in sympathy with the provision in the bill that
seeks to correct the abuse of short term credit granted by the
Federal reserve system to large banks. That there has been abuse no
one who has been observant would attempt to deny.[23]

As a result of the stock market crash and the continuing
deterioration of economic conditions, particular attention
was directed toward the interrelationship that had developed
between commercial and investment banking. Legislators
became convinced that the separation of such banking activities was essential. Of special interest were the complex
dealings between banking institutions and their security
affiliates. These companies, organized under state laws, engaged in a general securities business which included underwriting and the purchase and selling of stocks. Leading
bankers participated in the organization of such companies
so that they could partake of the highly profitable securities
business forbidden by the National Bank Act and by some
state laws. With the stock market crash of 1929, many of
these affiliates became drains on their parent banks. These
institutions, legal entities under state law, could only be
controlled by the federal government through prescribing
by law the exact relationship permitted between security
affiliates and the banks governed by federal legislation.

Some bankers recognized the dangers inherent in their
relationship to such companies. In response to a question
asked by Florida Democratic Senator Duncan Fletcher,
Rudolph Hecht the New Orleans banker replied, "I should
say that the tendency to limit the activities [of security
affiliate relationships] is perfectly correct." Hecht added,
however, that "the unscrambling of affiliate corporations,
which over a period of the last 15 years, have been closely
tied up with banking institutions appears to me to be very
difficult, and in some respects a dangerous procedure."[24]
This sentiment was echoed by O. Howard Wolfe, president

of the Association of Reserve City Bankers. Wolfe favored
the separation of commercial from investment banking, and
the divorcement of security affiliates, but feared "that at
the present time" it would have "a deflationary effect."[25]
William K. Payne, chairman of the Auburn-Cayuga National
Bank and Trust Company of Auburn, New York, voiced
the views of the small bankers when he said:

> We feel with a strong conviction that an attempt at this time to
> reform drastically, if you please, this branch of our financial
> system in the manner proposed by this bill would so inevitably
> and seriously affect security values that many of our small
> country banks, which have so far successfully weathered the
> storm would not be able to survive.[26]

His views were shared by McQuaid of the Barnett National
Bank in Jacksonville, Florida, who told the Senate committee
that they failed to recognize "the effect upon the general
banking structure of the country, and particularly the effect
upon country banks, outside of the cities in which security
markets are maintained."[27]

Investment bankers supported the continuance of security
affiliates. In 1932 the Investment Bankers Association passed
a resolution affirming "the existence of affiliates of banks
is necessary for the distribution of securities and the financing
of corporations."[28] After the stock market crash, the giants
of the security affiliate business were quick to defend their
operations, but, slowly, as conditions declined and banking
activities were increasingly scrutinized, banking institutions
reexamined their positions and gave their support to disaffiliation. This turn of events reached its climax with the announcement that the National City Company, affiliate of the
National City Bank, and the Chase Securities Company,
affiliate of the Chase National Bank, had determined on the
complete divorcement of the activities of these companies
from their parent banks. In the wake of the banking crisis,

the rising tide of public reaction made it impossible for Congress to do anything less than require complete divorcement of banks from their security affiliates.

As bank upon bank closed and depositors' funds were tied up in lengthy liquidation procedures, depositors demanded relief. Carter Glass opposed any form of government guarantee for deposits. Nevertheless, in its final form the Glass bill provided for the establishment of a Liquidation Corporation under which was to be developed a better system of receiverships so that depositors would have assurance that they would be able to obtain the liquidation of their claims upon the banks that closed. This plan, which was to be financed by contributions from member banks and the Federal Reserve System, gained a measure of support from the banking community. Many bankers, however, opposed the amount of assessed contributions proposed. Spenser S. Marsh, vice-president of the National Newark and Essex Banking Company of Newark, New Jersey, said: "We feel that it is too large an amount for medium size banks to contribute as an insurance fund, if we can use that term."[29] His views were shared by Rudolph Hecht, who pointed out that his objection to it "was more on the proportion of the Federal reserve contribution" which he felt would involve very little cash and "the banks who would have to put up a proportionately large amount."[30]

Although the proposed Liquidation Corporation was of concern to the banking community, the bankers gave far greater attention to the numerous bills introduced in Congress to provide for the guarantee of deposits. In 1932, Webster Bell, the president of the Maryland Bankers Association, told the membership of his organization that, at the request of the general counsel of the American Bankers Association, he had registered his protest on such legislation with the congressional representation from Maryland. He urged every member "to discuss the matter with our Mary-

land representatives at Washington without delay."[31] While
the Glass bill made no provision for deposit insurance, the
subject still came under discussion during the Senate hearings. When asked if he believed some guarantee should be
made to bank depositors, Percy H. Johnson of the Chemical
Bank and Trust Company of New York replied: "I do not
think so, unless we are going to guarantee all elements of
society against misfortunes and evils of all kinds. Of course,
if we are going to have socialistic government, then we
ought to guarantee everybody against all manner of things."[32]
In banking literature, proposals for deposit insurance were
repeatedly attacked. In April *The Southern Banker* commented on the quantity of bills introduced in Congress on
this subject:

> These bills constitute the most deadly threat that has been aimed at
> sound banking principles in this country. It behooves every banker
> to exercise the limit of his influence to forestall the passage of this
> or similar legislation. . . . While the motives of those advocating
> legislation of this character are above reproach, practical banking
> minds can see nothing less than disastrous consequences from the
> enactment of such legislation.[33]

In the spring of 1932, the House Banking and Currency
Committee held hearings on the Steagall deposit guarantee
bill. Supporters and opponents appeared before the members to argue their case. Of those who appeared, however,
only a handful were actively engaged in banking. The views
of the opposition were firmly voiced by Ronald Ransom,
president of the Georgia Bankers Association. Ransom
told the committee: "I do not believe there is any one subject that could be suggested to the Georgia bankers on which
there would be more unanimity than the subject of guaranty
of deposits. I will hazard the opinion that they are 100
percent opposed to it."[34] Ransom was joined in opposition
by A.L.M. Wiggins, president of the South Carolina Bankers

Association. Wiggins held that the enactment of deposit guarantee legislation would lead to panic. He said that the discussion of a bank guarantee law for the United States "accentuates, advertises, and puts in the public mind, from one end of the country to the other, the probability that the banking situation is a lot worse than they think it is." He felt that it would cause the public to "go to town and get their money out."[35]

Large banks in the commercial centers were totally opposed to the enactment of deposit guarantee plans. Confident of their own abilities to meet depositors' demands, they believed that the suggested plan would simply result in the large banks underwriting the losses of banks that were less sound. They held that losses to depositors of banks that failed would be covered by unlimited assessments on the open banks. Some bankers, however, supported the movement for deposit insurance. A. P. Fierson, vice-president of the East Tennessee National Bank of Knoxville, indicated that in view of "the conditions facing the financial structure today," he was confident that "it is imperative that we pass some form of legislation that will in some measure insure or guarantee the depositors' money in banks."[36] To bolster testimony of this nature, Chairman Steagall, author of the measure, inserted into the record of the hearings numerous letters which he had received from bankers and other individuals who favored the enactment of his bill.

In 1932, and throughout 1933, resistance to deposit insurance from the banking community held firm. With the avalanche of the banking crisis, public pressure gained strength, congressional and administration opposition weakened, and a deposit guarantee plan was enacted.

Throughout the Senate investigation, bankers fought against increased federal control over banking. This was evidenced in the movement against the extension of branch banking and in the objections raised to increasing the power of the Federal Reserve Board. Many bankers voiced opposition to the centralization of authority in Washington. Henry J. Haas, president of the American Bankers Association, told the Senate committee:

> We are of the opinion that it would be a serious mistake to pass a bill at this time having so many provisions of a deflationary and regulatory nature which would, in our opinion cause the withdrawal of a considerable number of members of the Federal reserve system. We believe that its effects would be injurious, not only to the member banks, but to the business interest of the country.[37]

Other bankers echoed this sentiment. Richard S. Hawes, president of the St. Louis Clearing House Association, spoke of the far-reaching character of the legislation. "To enact legislation which will so violently change the method of operation of banks," he said, "appears to me to be unwise."[38] James F. Burke, general counsel for the Pittsburgh Clearing House Association, presented a resolution passed by its membership. The resolution read in part.

> We are convinced also that the unprecedented centralization of authority in the Federal Reserve Board at Washington is certain to weaken, rather than strengthen, the banking structure, in addition to being in direct conflict with the constantly increasing opposition of the American people to the further absorption of local power and the assumption of purely local responsibilities by the Federal Government.[39]

Witness after witness appeared to offer testimony. All testimony followed the same line of thought: centralization was to be avoided and the times were too perilous for drastic legislative changes. Testimony was so consistent in its opposition that Senator Glass was moved to suggest that the witnesses must have been coached at night school to achieve such perfect unanimity of thought.[40]

Members of the banking community were joined by the
Federal Reserve banks in opposing centralization of power
in Washington. Leadership in this movement was taken by
the Federal Reserve Bank of New York. Governor George L.
Harrison informed the executive committee of the board
of directors of the bank that the fundamental objection to
the Glass bill was the concentration of authority in Washington, not only with respect to Federal Reserve banks, but to
member banks as well. He feared, however, that Senator
Glass would view this opposition with suspicion and would
consider such objections to be arguments for the concentration of power in New York rather than sound economic arguments. He thought that the "present mood" of Congress
made it useless to argue the point.[41] Nevertheless, with the
full approval of the board of directors of the New York Bank,
Harrison sent a lengthy letter to Senator Peter Norbeck,
chairman of the Senate Banking and Currency Committee,
expressing the views of the Reserve Bank:

> The bill through many of its provisions tends further to centralize
> in the Federal Reserve Board the control of operations of the
> Federal Reserve banks and the member banks. We believe in the
> basic principle of the Federal reserve act that the public interest
> will be best served by leaving to the boards of directors of the
> several federal reserve banks autonomous powers of operations
> within the terms of the law, and by leaving to the Federal Reserve
> board general and broad powers of supervision as was always
> contemplated by the framers of the Federal reserve act.[42]

Harrison's letter drew a sharp retort from Senator Glass:

> You may be sure that I am in nowise astonished at the nature of
> the letter nor at the approval of the New York Board. I am,
> however, distinctly gratified, as I feel confident our committee
> will be, that you and your board have thus stated in unequivocal
> terms the misconception of the Federal Reserve banking act which
> so long has been reflected in the extraordinary policies pursued

by the New York bank with respect to both domestic and foreign transactions. It is truly a notable document. In my considered view it constitutes a challenge to statutory authority and an un-yielding antagonism to any restraining influence whatsoever.

For my part the challenge will be squarely met and the issue distinctly joined in the United States Senate.[43]

In turn, Harrison replied:

I am greatly puzzled as to what you mean when you refer to the "extraordinary policies pursued by the New York bank with respect to both domestic and foreign transactions," and also your reaction that our document "represents an unyielding antagonism to any restraining influence whatsoever." Nothing in my letter was intended to resist appropriate restraint of credit. It was rather proposed to express our sincere and earnest opinion as to the wisdom of one form of restraint as compared with another. If by restraining influence you mean restraint of individual reserve bank powers, I can only say that we have never believed in an uncon-trolled autonomy in the several reserve banks but that, on the other hand, we do foresee possible serious disadvantages to the country in too great a centralization of those powers in any one institution, whether in New York or in Washington.[44]

Although the Reserve banks did not favor centralization of power in Washington, they did support the establishment of a unified system of commercial banking in the United States. Their views were shared by the Federal Reserve Board. Eugene Meyer told the Senate Banking and Currency Subcommittee that "effective supervision of banking in this country has been seriously affected by the competition between member and nonmember banks." He felt that "branch banking under a unified system would meet with a great deal of support." Questioned about the constitutionality of such a system, Meyer answered that he did not think there was any doubt about the ability to do it. "The principal thing about being able to do something is to want to do it," he affirmed. In response, Senator Glass said: "I think the curse of the banking system of this country is the dual system." He then suggested that the subject be investigated by the Federal Reserve Board and that a memorandum be prepared concerning the constitutionality of the question.[45]

As a result of this exchange of views, Walter Wyatt, general counsel for the Reserve Board, made a detailed exploration of the constitutionality of unification of commercial banks into one system under federal law. His resulting memorandum was forwarded to the Senate Banking and Currency Subcommittee in December 1932.[46] It was made public in the days immediately following the banking crisis.

The advantages of a unified banking system were recognized by some members of the banking community. O. H. Wolfe, president of the Association of Reserve City Bankers, told the Senate subcommittee: "I believe we ought to force into the Federal Reserve system, if we can, every bank that does a commercial business, whether State or national bank." He did not know, however, how this could be accomplished.[47] W. R. McQuaid spoke of the difficulties of the dual banking system. He pointed out that "part of our trouble is very largely because there are 48 systems outside the Federal reserve" with "different kinds of regulations." McQuaid was asked for his views on how to rectify the situation. He indicated that passage of a provision for statewide branch banking would lead to a uniform system of banking if the Federal Reserve System were made "attractive to the banks that do come into the system."[48]

Central bank advocates called for complete government ownership of the banking system. These supporters, primarily belonging to the Progressive and Socialist movements, found little support in the banking community, Congress, or the administration. There was no widespread demand by the public for such action. Nonetheless, in some areas of the country, deposits were withdrawn from banks

and redeposited in the Postal Savings System, an action
evidencing the depositors' greater faith in government institutions than in their local banks. Bankers feared the growth
of this movement and its subsequent impact on demands
for increased government control of the banking system.
They were, therefore, quick to protest against what they
considered unfair competition from the federal government.

Supporters of the dual banking system offered alterna-
tives to proposals for increased federal control over banking.
In January 1933, *The Bankers Magazine* called for the
betterment of the state banking system, and stated editorially: "There is nothing except the will of the people
to prevent States from having the best banking systems
assured by any laws or any system of official supervision."[49]
One month later, that same publication carried a proposal
for adopting a uniform state banking code; such a code
would be enacted by individual state legislatures and would
thus obviate the necessity for increased federal control
over banking.[50]

As banking problems multiplied, bankers were warned of
the possibility of government control. Albert C. Agnew,
general counsel for the Federal Reserve Bank of San Francisco, addressed the California bankers: "Either the bankers
of this country will realize that they are guardians of the
moneys committed to their charge, and will conduct themselves accordingly, or banking will cease to be a private
enterprise and will become a purely government function."
He pointed out that the lack of a nationwide policy on
banking had resulted in "a hodge-podge of banking which is
the root of our difficulty."[51]

Banking in the United States had indeed become a "hodge-
podge." Self-interest, concern for local conditions, fear of
change, and lack of unity—all contributed to the fact that
banking problems had mushroomed and were creating a

national crisis. Bankers as a group offered few remedies for
the critical economic situation of which they were so vital
a part. Too close to their own local problems, few bankers
were able to achieve an overall view of banking conditions.
Those who did were voices crying in the wilderness. Because
of their inability to evolve a unified plan of action to correct
banking abuses, bankers were unprepared to cope with
the declining situation. It is not surprising then that they
made few positive contributions to the bank reform legislation enacted during the first hundred days of the
Roosevelt administration.

NOTES

1. Gerald Fischer, *American Banking Structure* (New York, 1968), pp. 42-53.

2. U.S. Comptroller of the Currency, *Annual Report, December 1, 1930*
(Washington, D.C., 1931), p. 1.

3. U.S. Secretary of the Treasury, *Annual Report June 30, 1931* (Washington, D.C., 1932), pp. 34-35.

4. U.S. House of Representatives, Banking and Currency Committee, 71st
Congress, 2d Session, *Branch, Chain and Group Banking, Hearings . . . under
H.R. 141,* 2 vols. (Washington, D.C., 1930), I, p. 1537.

5. U.S. Senate, Banking and Currency Committee, 72d Congress, 1st
Session, *Operations of the National and Federal Reserve Banking System,
Hearings . . . on S4115,* 2 pts. (Washington, D.C., 1932), II, p. 298. (Hereafter
referred to as U.S. Senate, Banking and Currency Committee, Hearings *S4115.*)

6. U.S. Senate, Banking and Currency Subcommittee, 71st Congress, 3d
Session, *Operations of the National and Federal Reserve Banking Systems.
Hearings Pursuant to S. Res. 71,* 7 pts. (Washington, D.C., 1931), II, p. 324.
(Hereafter referred to as U.S. Senate, Banking and Currency Subcommittee,
Hearings S. Res. 71.)

7. U.S. Senate, Banking and Currency Committee, *Hearings S.4115,* II,
p. 306.

8. Ibid., p. 248.

9. Ibid., pp. 327-328.

10. U.S. Senate, Banking and Currency Subcommittee, *Hearings S. Res. 71,*
I, pp. 269-270.

11. Ibid., p. 195.

12. U.S. Senate, Banking and Currency Committee, *Hearings S.4115,* II, p. 356.

13. *The Southern Banker,* LXII (August 1932), p. 46.

14. *The New York Times,* January 15, 1933.

15. *The Texas Bankers Record,* XXII (January 1933), p. III.

16. National Association of Supervisors of State Banks, *Proceedings of 29th Annual Convention* (n.p., 1930), p. 23.

17. Ibid., *Proceedings of the 30th Annual Convention* (n.p., 1931), p. 19.

18. Ibid., *Proceedings of the 31st Annual Convention* (n.p., 1932), p. 29.

19. Federal Reserve Board, *Sixteenth Annual Report* (Washington, D.C., 1930), pp. 3-4.

20. Investment Bankers Association of America, *Proceedings of the 20th Annual Convention* (Chicago, 1931), p. 5.

21. Ibid., *Proceedings of the 21st Annual Convention* (Chicago, 1932), pp. 8-9.

22. U.S. Senate, Banking and Currency Committee, *Hearings S.4115,* II, p. 286.

23. Ibid., p. 305.

24. Ibid., p. 231.

25. Ibid., p. 267.

26. Ibid., p. 329.

27. Ibid., p. 279.

28. Waldo Kendall to Carter Glass, May 18, 1932, Box 304, Carter Glass Papers, Alderman Library, University of Virginia. (Hereafter referred to as Glass Papers.)

29. U.S. Senate, Banking and Currency Committee, *Hearings S.4115,* II, p. 299.

30. Ibid., p. 238.

31. Maryland Bankers Association, *Proceedings of the Annual Convention, 1932* (Baltimore, Md., 1932), p. 12.

32. U.S. Senate, Banking and Currency Committee, *Hearings S.4115,* I, p. 160.

33. *The Southern Banker,* LXIII (April 1932), p. 18.

34. U.S. House of Representatives, Banking and Currency Subcommittee, 72d Congress, 1st Session, *To Provide a Guaranty Fund for Depositors in Banks, Hearings . . . H.R. (10241) 11362* (Washington, D.C., 1932), p. 170.

35. Ibid., p. 232.

36. Ibid., p. 58.

37. U.S. Senate, Banking and Currency Committee, *Hearings S. 4115,* I, p. 59.

38. Ibid., p. 176.

39. Ibid., II, p. 442.

40. Ibid., pp. 386, 436.

41. Federal Reserve Bank of New York, Board of Directors, Executive Committee, Memorandum of Meeting, March 29, 1932, "Discussion Notes," Harrison Papers.

42. U.S. Senate, Banking and Currency Committee, *Hearings S.4115,* II, pp. 499-500.

43. Glass to Harrison, April 9, 1932, Box 272, Glass Papers.

44. Harrison to Glass, April 18, 1932, Ibid.

45. U.S. Senate, Banking and Currency Committee, *Hearings S. 4115*, II, p. 395.

46. *Federal Reserve Bulletin*, XIX (March 1933), pp. 166-168.

47. U.S. Senate, Banking and Currency Committee, *Hearings S.4115*, II, p. 277.

48. Ibid., pp. 292-293.

49. *The Bankers Magazine*, CXXVI (January 1933), p. 4.

50. Ibid., (February 1933):308.

51. Albert C. Agnew, "Some Thoughts About the Future of American Banking," *The California Banker*, XIV (June 1933), pp. 194-195.

4

The Banking Act of 1933 and the Failure of the Opposition

The passage of the Emergency Banking Act and the reopening of the banks solved the immediate banking crisis, but the problem of remedial bank reform legislation remained. Franklin Roosevelt's original plan was to summon the legislators, enact the emergency program, and then recess Congress until comprehensive economic reforms could be formulated. Public reaction to the bank holiday was so favorable, however, that the administration decided to proceed with additional legislation designed to aid not only the banking situation, but overall economic conditions as well. In a letter to a Massachusetts banker, the president wrote: "We seem to be off to a good start and I hope to get through some important legislation while the feeling of the country is so friendly."[1]

On March 10, the president sent his second message to Congress. He asked for curtailment in government spending by reducing veterans' pensions and government salaries. The Economy Act was passed on March 20. Although the atmosphere was optimistic, the president was keenly aware of the problems that lay ahead, and he understood well the attitude that the banking community would take toward many of his proposals. After the passage of the Economy Act, Roosevelt wrote to Colonel Edward M. House, Woodrow Wilson's adviser.

> While things look superficially rosy, I realize well that this far [sic]
> we have actually given more of deflation than of inflation—the
> closed banks locked up four billion or more, and the economy legis-
> lation will take nearly another billion out of veterans' pay, depart-
> mental salaries, etc. It is simply inevitable that we must inflate and
> though my banker friends may be horrified, I am still seeking an
> inflation which will not wholly be based on additional government
> debt.[2]

In the first days following the enactment of the bank emergency program, the president made no direct move toward
overall bank reform legislation. But action could not be
avoided or long delayed, for the administration was faced
with the immediate impact of an intense public indignation
directed against bankers and banking practices. Early in 1933,
as the Senate debated the Glass bill and the House considered
the guarantee of bank deposits, investigations into stock
market practices were held. Leading bankers appeared before
the Senate investigating subcommittee, and disclosed their
participation in speculative ventures. In February, as bank
after bank closed, testimony was given under the relentless
probing of Ferdinand Pecora, newly appointed counsel to
the Senate subcommittee. The revelations made shocked the
public. Well-known bankers had engaged in unsavory practices; bad judgment, irresponsible personal gain, and betrayal
of the public trust characterized their activities. The climax
came with the revelation that two giants of the New York
banking world, Charles E. Mitchell of the National City Bank
and Albert H. Wiggin of the Chase National Bank, had, for a
period of years, successfully evaded the payment of income
taxes. Disclosures concerning the activities of other bankers
soon followed. Public reaction was vehement.

The combination of events—the crisis and the scandalous
disclosures—brought forth demands for bank reform from
the press, the public, and members of Congress. William
Gibbs McAdoo, newly elected senator from California, and

secretary of the Treasury under Woodrow Wilson, voiced the views of many when he stated:

> The credit structure of the U.S. is a disgraceful failure, our entire banking system does credit to a collection of imbeciles. . . . I favor a constitutional amendment that will deprive all States of the power of creating and controlling banks, and that will put one federal banking system into effect which will make every bank in the nation safe.[3]

Mirroring public opinion, the press scorned the bankers and called for immediate reform. *The Literary Digest* reported that "the restoration of justified instead of misplaced confidence in our banking system is the commanding need of the hour."[4] *Business Week* stated that "sincere advocates of banking reform hope the Administration will be able to push its measures through with great promptness before the forces of opposition have time to rally."[5] Other periodicals and newspapers reflected similar views.

While rumors flourished, legislators acted. On March 11, two days after the enactment of the Emergency Banking Act, Senator Glass introduced a measure which closely resembled the Glass banking bill considered by the old Congress. He indicated that he hoped this bill "might be the basis for permanent legislation."[6] On March 14, Senator Thomas P. Gore, Democrat from Oklahoma, introduced a joint resolution calling for a constitutional amendment that would give Congress control over all banking in the United States.[7] Reports were that the Federal Reserve Board had transmitted to the Senate Banking and Currency Committee the draft of a bill providing for the establishment of a uniform commercial banking system in the United States. Credence was given to this report with the publication of the Wyatt memorandum supporting the constitutionality of such a system under federal law which had been prepared at the request of Senator Glass during the banking hearings of the previous Congress.[8]

In mid-March President Roosevelt turned his attention to permanent banking legislation. A conference was called at the White House attended by Treasury officials, representatives of the Federal Reserve Board, and Senator Glass. At the conclusion of the meeting, it was reported that at least some "phase of banking legislation would be advanced," and that the Glass banking bill would be "made the immediate vehicle for a portion of the permanent banking reform." It was stressed that the immediate aim of the administration would be to get the banking system back on its feet as rapidly as possible, while the larger objective would be "to get a permanently united and coherent banking system through the Federal Reserve system."[9]

Meanwhile, Carter Glass sent a copy of the "so called Glass banking bill" to the president.[10] For six weeks numerous conferences were held. Consultations took place between congressional leaders and members of the administration. The press noted the frequent visits of Senator Glass to the office of the president. It was reported that Democratic Senator Duncan Fletcher, the new chairman of the Senate Banking and Currency Committee, and Chairman Steagall of the House Banking and Currency Committee had been called to the White House. No official statements were made, but press opinion held that the decision lay in purifying the existing banking system rather than eliminating it.

Rumors and conjectures regarding the various agreements and disagreements continued to abound. *Business Week* stressed the importance of the deposit insurance question, stating: "Washington does not remember any issue on which sentiment of the country has been so undivided or emphatically expressed as this." It was further reported that Senator Glass had yielded and written it into his bill because "the public demand is so strong."[11] *The New York Times* indicated that the president was dissatisfied with the deposit insurance proposal and desired time to

study the question.[12] Other differences were reported to
have arisen. Secretary Woodin was said to be insisting that
the secretary of the Treasury remain a member of the Federal
Reserve Board, while Senator Glass, a former secretary of
the Treasury was known to advocate the elimination of this
ex officio member from the board.[13] Branch banking remained
an issue. The president was said to favor countywide rather
than statewide extension of branches. Others, including Carter
Glass, favored a more liberal policy.[14]

Letters poured into the White House and to congressional
offices from bankers and from the general public. Finally,
on May 10, Senator Glass introduced a revised version of his
banking bill. It was immediately referred to the Senate Banking and Currency Committee.[15] One week later, on May 17,
Representative Steagall introduced a similar bill in the House
of Representatives.[16] These measures provided for numerous
changes in the banking structure. They called for an increase
in Federal Reserve control over credit operations, its extension
to member banks and to the Federal Reserve banks. Provision
was made for the coordination of Federal Reserve open market
operations, and statutory recognition was given to the Open
Market Committee. Supervision of all Federal Reserve foreign
operations was placed directly under the control of the
Federal Reserve Board. Commercial banking was separated
from investment banking. Commercial banks were no longer
permitted to underwrite securities other than those issued
by state and local governments, and member banks were
required to divorce themselves from their security affiliates
within one year. Private banks were forced to choose between
deposit banking and investment banking. National banks were
permitted to establish branches on a statewide basis in those
states that extended the privilege to state banks. Control over
chain and group banking was provided by regulating the right
of holding company affiliates of federally supervised banks
to vote stock held in such banks. The capital requirements for

national banks was increased, and provision was made for
the establishment of a Federal Deposit Insurance Corporation.

Throughout the spring of 1933, the attitudes and actions
of the banking community were greatly influenced by the
impact of the banking crisis. In April 1933, the Economic
Policy Commission of the American Bankers Association
proposed a series of significant changes for the nation's
banking structure. Support was given to granting increased
power to the Federal Reserve Board. In reviewing the
banking crisis, the commission reported that "probably
the most astonishing and disappointing feature of the bank
crisis was the demonstrated impotence of the Federal Reserve System to retain control of the situation." In its report
the commission suggested: "Perhaps a solution is to be
sought in the formation of a Central Bank of the United
States with the present Reserve Banks as branches. If that
does not appear to be the wise solution then a better one
must be found for the dangers inherent in the present arrangement have been all too fully demonstrated." The commission called for the immediate enactment of the revised
Glass banking bill and said that "the Federal Administration
should create a commission to recommend after mature
deliberation, the further changes that should be made in our
Federal Reserve system and in our monetary system."[17]

State bankers continued to oppose any abrogation of states'
rights. In Des Moines, Iowa, a conference of banking com-
missioners and the officials of fourteen midwestern bankers
associations met and adopted a resolution calling for the
"recognition of the right of the states to maintain their own
banking systems." They also recommended that "the President appoint a commission to study and propose basic changes
in the dual banking system."[18] During this period a number
of state bankers associations held their annual meetings. The
proposed changes in the banking laws under consideration
by Congress were discussed. Nathan Adams of the First

National Bank of Dallas, Texas, addressed the Georgia Bankers Association and commented on the move to increase the power of the Federal Reserve Board:

> I yield to no man in my admiration for the fundamental principles of the Federal Reserve banking system, which I contend are the discounting of paper, the issuance of currency based on the provisions of the act, open market transactions and assisting in government financing. Beyond these prerogatives any power conferred upon the Federal Reserve Board is purely a political power usurping the constitutional rights of those banks which own the capital of the Federal Reserve Banks.[19]

Other bankers shared this view. In May, M. E. Holderness, president of the Missouri Bankers Association, told the members of that organization that "many of our accepted principles of individualism and free initiative are not only being attacked but are steadily being forced to give way before an increased demand for more centralized control." He did not take issue with the enacted emergency measures, but felt that the bankers should see to it that "there are no repercussions in these emergency acts." He said:

> We must replace the temporary measures with permanent legislation, but we must not erect prejudice into accepted financial principles nor federal law. . . . It seems to me an unassailable proposition that the successful bankers of America should be permitted, out of their experience, to perform a logical and useful service by advising in the construction of the new American banking system.

Holderness saw "no ultimate alternative for banking but the adoption of a unified system," and believed that such a system would have "nothing at variance or in conflict with the interest of independent banking." He contemplated "no abandonment of the state banking systems," but he believed that "a unified system should help eliminate the hazards which undesirable competition between the two systems introduces."[20]

The same problems were discussed at other state bankers

conventions. In California J. F. Sullivan, Jr., vice-president of the Crocker-First National Bank of San Francisco, addressed the California Bankers Association. He indicated that part of their program for better banking called for "improvements in the banking systems of the State and Country."

> Many fundamental changes are now in progress of legislation but most of these proposals have been the spawn of political agitators and not of banking leaders. We welcome changes that will actually strengthen the banking system; that will safeguard its solvency, assure its careful supervision and develop its efficient operation. Such changes should be made, however, after thorough and mature deliberation, and should supplement the emergency banking legislation enacted hastily during the banking holiday.

Sullivan believed that the Federal Reserve Board was "the logical body in which to repose "banking authority." He felt that "it would seem to be entirely practical and desirable that in the near future all bank charters, both State and national, should be granted only by and with the approval of the Federal Reserve Board."[21] Such action was supported by *The Magazine of Wall Street,* which commented: "We have too many banks and too divergent policies of government control." It recommended that "the first remedy is to force all sound banks into a unified system of Federal control, a structure for which is already established in the Federal Reserve System."[22] Centralization under Federal Reserve control also gained the support of the New York State banking authorities. The State Banking Board sent a resolution to Congress favoring compulsory membership in the Federal Reserve System for all banks and trust companies.[23]

The upheavals in the banking world had altered the views of many bankers, and new voices were replacing those of discredited bankers. In March, Winthrop W. Aldrich, the new chairman of the governing board of the Chase National Bank, issued a statement on the security operations of banks. He stated that "the spirit of speculation should be eradicated from the management of commercial banks." Aldrich noted that "commercial banks should not be permitted to underwrite securities, except securities of the United States Government and of the states, territories, municipalities and certain other public bodies in the United States."[24] Shortly thereafter, it was announced that the Chase National Bank would set in motion an immediate separation from its affiliated security corporation. This step followed closely upon similar steps taken by the National City Bank under the leadership of its new president, James Perkins. The action taken by these two banks did much to undermine the resistance of the banking community to the divorcement of security affiliates. The speed with which disaffiliation was accomplished was noted by the Congress and was reflected in the proposed legislation that imposed a one-year limit for other banks to achieve similar action. Some resistance remained. Allan M. Pope of the First of Boston Corporation wrote to Senator Fletcher and urged that Congress allow at least two years for banks to comply with the law.[25] Other bankers took similar action.

The proposed creation of a Federal Deposit Insurance Corporation was the most controversial feature of the new banking legislation. The bills, as introduced in both the House and the Senate, provided that the corporation be financed by assessments levied on the banks applying for membership and on the twelve Federal Reserve banks. In addition, the federal government initially was to contribute the sum of $150 million. However, under the proposal, the corporation would not begin operations until July 1, 1934. Many legislators felt strongly that an immediate guarantee of deposits was necessary. On May 19, Senator Arthur Vandenberg, Republican from Michigan, introduced an amendment supporting this position. Upon offering the amendment, he said:

I happen to be one of those who hold firmly to the view that there is no remote possibility of adequate and competent economic recuperation in the United States during the next 12 months, regardless of all the other splendid undertakings which may be underway, until confidence in normal banking is restored; and in the face of existing circumstances I am perfectly sure that the insurance of bank deposits immediately is the paramount and fundamental necessity of the moment.[26]

The Vandenberg amendment called for the insurance of small deposit accounts in banks. The plan was to be financed by the federal government and was to begin immediately, continuing until the establishment of the permanent Deposit Insurance Corporation. On May 20, the House of Representatives took up the Steagall bill; after debate it was passed on May 23.[27] Meanwhile, in the Senate debate continued on the Glass bill. On May 26, it too was approved, with the Vandenberg amendment included in the measure.[28]

As the remedial banking legislation moved through Congress, bankers voiced their objections to many provisions of the bill. Out of favor with the public, out of harmony with the new administration, and disunited within the banking field itself, their opposition had little impact on the course of the legislative measure. On the subject of deposit insurance, however, they were united. Many believed it was inherently unsound. Others felt it was oppressively unfair, that it forced the good to pay for the bad and would further weaken the banking structure of the nation.

At bankers' conventions, in public addresses, and in the financial press, bankers were pressed to take up the fight against deposit insurance. *The Bankers Magazine* stated:

The first task of Government in reforming the banking system should be to insure the soundness and suitability of the assets of banks. If this aim is accomplished guaranty of deposits is uncalled for. If this is not accomplished guaranty provisions would be unjustified, inequitable, and very possibly unworkable.[29]

As Congress considered the banking bill, bankers continued to air their views on deposit insurance. Francis Sissons, president of the American Bankers Association, praised the bank reform efforts, but condemned the deposit insurance aspect of the bills.[30] In an article in *The Bankers Magazine,* he stressed the fact that the plan incorporated in the Glass bill was "not essentially different from that tried in the States." He held that "a very thorough reorganization, consolidation and strengthening of the bank supervisional field in this country is called for," but he denied that deposit insurance gave "the public real protection for their deposits.[31] The Pennsylvania Bankers Association adopted a resolution opposing the deposit insurance proposal.[32] Similar action was taken by the New Jersey Bankers Association.[33] Winthrop W. Aldrich of the Chase National Bank voiced his opposition to this feature of the banking bill. In a letter to President Roosevelt, he wrote of the "unfortunate consequences that would ensue." He suggested amendments to the initial capital contributions required, stating that as it now stood the measure "would place an unbearable burden on the capital structure of the banks of the country." He believed that this requirement should be tied in to a reduction of the rate of interest paid on time deposits to "place on depositors a proper share of the expense of deposit insurance."[34] Aldrich was supported by other bankers and bankers associations. The members of the Boston Clearing House Association unanimously voted to record their opposition to the deposit insurance provisions of the proposed legislation, on the ground that deposit insurance was "economically unsound, both theoretically and as demonstrated by experience."[35] Comparable action was taken by the Fort Worth Clearing House Association.[36] The Missouri Bankers Association empowered the president of that organization to appoint two representatives to go to Washington, at the association's expense, for the purpose of opposing a bank guarantee law "if passage seemed imminent."[37]

The Federal Reserve banks were equally concerned with the deposit insurance feature of the bank reform bills. In April Secretary Woodin attended a meeting of the executive committee of the board of directors of the Federal Reserve Bank of New York, and inquired as to the committee's reaction to deposit insurance. Clearly the committee was opposed. Owen D. Young felt it would only be valid in the case of national banks since they were the only banks over which the federal government had exclusive supervision. He thought that to guarantee bank deposits in institutions where control could not be exercised was unreasonable. If the deposits in state banks were guaranteed, Young believed, the drive toward a unified banking system would be weakened. However, he did see political and psychological advantages to deposit insurance if it were limited to national banks. Other committee members supported these views. Governor Harrison observed that the adoption of piecemeal legislation enacted in the past to meet special situations had been the cause of many problems. He warned that, in view of the banking emergency, such steps might now be taken. He advised against further tinkering and recommended that intense study be given to devising legislation for a fundamental revision of the banking system. Only then, he believed, would it be possible to determine the proper role for a federal guarantee of bank deposits. Under the existing conditions he did not think it possible to get sound deposit guarantee legislation.[38]

Discussion of deposit insurance continued at subsequent meetings of the directors of the Federal Reserve Bank of New York. On May 4, the topic was again considered. It was the view of George W. Davison that the proposal was wholly impracticable. He was particularly concerned that the banks of the country could not assume the obligations contemplated in the measure before Congress.[39] On June 1,

Governor Harrison reported to the directors that an alternate plan had been recommended by the Federal Reserve Bank of New York, and had been submitted by the Treasury Department to the appropriate congressional committee and rejected. The plan proposed that RFC loans to banks would be liberalized and that loans under Section 10b of the Federal Reserve Act would be made by Federal Reserve banks with government guarantee against loss. This was to be combined with some relaxation of the existing membership requirement. Harrison pointed out that the administration had not committed itself on the deposit guarantee provision of the pending banking legislation; he noted that its preference was for a solution to the banking difficulties along the lines of the proposal made by the Federal Reserve Bank of New York, the Treasury Department, and the RFC. Harrison thought there might still be a chance that this proposal would be adopted. He indicated that Senator Glass did not want any substantial alterations in his bill which would delay or prevent its passage. It was Harrison's opinion, however, that the only recourse was for the president to tell Glass he was opposed to the guarantee of bank deposits and that he would veto the Glass-Steagall bill unless that provision were eliminated and something appropriate substituted; only then might Glass agree, since he was not a supporter of deposit insurance.[40]

Although the protest of the banking community continued, public demand for deposit insurance increased. Originally, deposit insurance was not part of the administration's program. Roosevelt, however, astute politician that he was, did not underestimate the power of the people. As early as March 12, he had been reliably advised that twenty-five Democratic members of the House had signed a caucus petition in support of a government guarantee for bank deposits.[41] Prior to the introduction of the Banking Act of 1933, while negotiations were underway to

reconcile differences of opinion on bank reform, it was
reported that the president had suggested deferment of the
insurance feature for one year to give the banking situation
time to clarify, and to permit the close examination of all
the banks eligible to join the insurance plan. Senator Glass,
it was reported, had "told the White House and the Treasury
that if he [Glass] didn't write it into the bill Congress
would."[42] Finally, at the president's suggestion, the Banking
and Currency Committee of the Senate provided for the
insurance of time and demand deposits on a graduated basis—
100 percent insurance of accounts up to $10,000, 74 percent
for accounts from $10,000 to $50,000, and 50 percent for
accounts exceeding $50,000.[43] If it was with reluctance
that the president accepted the deposit insurance provisions
set forth in the legislation, he was completely opposed to
the Vandenberg amendment which provided for the immediate guarantee of bank deposits. *The New York Times*
reported that he had notified Senator Glass and Representative Steagall that he would veto the bill if the Vandenberg
amendment was retained.[44] Conferences and consultations
resulted. It was rumored that the Vandenberg amendment
was "completely unacceptable" to Secretary Woodin but
that Roosevelt knew there were "votes enough in both the
Senate and House to pass any deposit insurance plan." It was
also rumored that Senator Vandenberg had said "that if his
measure [was] stricken from the bank bill he [would] tack it
as a rider to the next administration program and force a vote
on it."[45] Senator Glass, meanwhile, warned the president
of the folly of delay. Fearing the consequences of additional
debate, Glass referred to Huey Long's filibuster in the previous
session, pointing out that if action was not taken "the time
of your Administration will be taken up in its early stages
with a repetition of the disgraceful spectacle we have recently had in the Senate." He believed that another epidemic
of bank failures would follow if the bill failed.[46]

While the debate on deposit insurance raged, the president continued to study the problem. On June 6, in reply to a letter from a New England banker who protested this feature of the bill, Roosevelt wrote: "There seems to be no question that we shall have some form of bank insurance. I am trying to have it made as sound as possible."[47] In a similar letter he told Clark Howell, editor of the *Atlanta Constitution:* "You are quite right about the bank insurance provision as it passed the Senate. I am doing everything possible to correct it."[48] After considerable negotiations, a compromise was finally reached. The president agreed to accept the Vandenberg amendment if the effective date were postponed until January 1, 1934, but he also agreed to approve a provision that would empower him to fix by proclamation an earlier date for the beginning of deposit insurance should he deem it necessary. This compromise was accepted by the House and Senate members of the conference committee when they met to iron out the differences between the banking bills passed by their respective chambers.

A second compromise was reached by the conferees. In the final analysis the Senate version of the Banking Act of 1933 differed from that of the House in its approach to eligible membership in the Federal Deposit Insurance Corporation. Congressman Steagall had insisted that state member banks be allowed to join the Corporation, regardless of their membership in the Federal Reserve System. The House bill reflected his position. Carter Glass saw the Corporation as a means whereby state banks could be forced to become members of the Federal Reserve System. He had insisted upon the inclusion of this provision in the Senate bill. The Conference Report recommended that state banks which were not members of the Federal Reserve System should be permitted to join the Federal Deposit Insurance Corporation, with the proviso that they would become members of the system by July 1, 1936.[49]

On June 13, 1933, the report of the conference committee was submitted in both houses of Congress. Senator Glass reported to the Senate that "98 percent of the bill remained as it had been originally passed by the Senate." He noted the adjustment to the Vandenberg amendment, indicating that the change had been made at the insistence of the administration.[50] Chairman Steagall called up the Conference Report in the House of Representatives. He stated that the bill embodied "without substantial change the regulatory provisions of what was originally known as the Glass bill which passed the Senate in a former session of Congress, but failed of passage in the House, together with a provision for the insurance of bank deposits."[51] In both houses debate was brief, the Conference Report was accepted, and a banking bill was finally approved by the Congress. Three days later, on June 16, 1933, the president signed the new banking act into law.[52] He congratulated Carter Glass as "father of the best piece of banking legislation since his other law creating the Federal Reserve System."[53] The president was indeed right, for it was, in truth, the only major comprehensive banking measure enacted since the Federal Reserve Act of 1913.

Differences of opinion on bank reform had not subsided, but federal control over American banking had been advanced. According to *The Literary Digest,* "The Glass Steagall Banking bill does more than bring American bankers to the fork in the road of business practices. It puts them down in the midst of what is almost a maze of paths to the future."[54] The Banking Act of 1933 was designed to tighten the loopholes in the American banking structure. It provided for a more rigid control over capital requirements and the investment policies of federally supervised banks. It was to have an impact on all state banks while at the same time preserving their independence of the Federal Reserve System. As a result of popular pressure, it established a deposit insurance plan that neither the president, the Senate-sponsor of the bill, nor the bankers desired, and it laid the foundation for far-reaching changes in American banking.

In an address to the New York State Bankers Association, Adolf Berle, a presidential adviser, stressed that the Glass-Steagall Act would only be regarded as a "bridge or a transition rather than as a permanent solution for the situation." He called upon the bankers as a group "to give some evidence of desiring to improve the system as a whole rather than furthering their own particular interests."[55] For their part bankers continued to debate the question of bank reform legislation. Their immediate concern was the plan for deposit insurance. As the future unfolded, their efforts would effect the postponement of the plan and would bring about readjustments in the assessments levied on the banks. But in time this fight would lose its force and banker opposition would center on the broader issues of monetary management and credit control. Designed as remedial legislation and born in the throes of the depression, the Banking Act of 1933 left much to be desired. Neither the administration nor the banking community was satisfied with its accomplishments. In the period that lay ahead, both would reconsider banking legislation and plans would evolve to provide for a fuller solution to the banking problems in the United States.

NOTES

1. Elliott Roosevelt, ed., *F.D.R.: His Personal Letters, 1905-1945,* 4 vols. (New York, 1947-1950), III, p. 338. (Hereafter referred to as *F.D.R. Personal Letters.*)

2. Roosevelt to House, April 5, 1933, President's Personal Files, Folder 222, Roosevelt Papers.

3. *Time,* XXI (February 27, 1933), p. 18.

4. *The Literary Digest,* CXV (March 18, 1933), p. 12.

5. *Business Week,* March 15, 1933, p. 4.

6. *Congressional Record,* LXXVII, p. 196.

7. Ibid., p. 246.

8. *The New York Times,* March 15, 1933.

9. Ibid., March 30, 1933.

10. Glass to Roosevelt, March 24, 1933, Box 6 Glass Papers.

11. *Business Week,* April 12, 1933.

12. *The New York Times,* April 12, 1933.

13. Ibid., April 22, 1933.

14. Ibid., April 12, 1933.

15. *Congressional Record,* LXXVII, p. 3109.

16. Ibid., p. 3611.

17. American Bankers Association, "Report of the Economic Policy Commission," April 10-12, 1933, President's Official File 230, Box 1, Roosevelt Papers.

18. Iowa Bankers Association to Roosevelt, April 22, 1933, ibid.

19. *The Southern Banker,* LX (June 1933), p. 18.

20. Missouri Bankers Association, *Proceedings of the Forty-third Annual Convention* (St. Louis, Mo., 1933), pp. 26-29.

21. California Bankers Association, "Complete Proceedings, 1933 Convention," *The California Banker,* XIV (June 1933), pp. 180-184.

22. *The Magazine of Wall Street,* LI (April 15, 1933), p. 656.

23. Ibid.

24. Winthrop W. Aldrich, *Suggestions for Improving the Banking System* (n.p., 1933), pp. 6-7.

25. Pope to Fletcher, April 10, 1933, Box 311, Glass Papers.

26. *Congressional Record,* LXXVII, p. 3731.

27. Ibid., p. 4058.

28. Ibid., p. 4182.

29. Frederick A. Bradford, "Futility of Deposit Guaranty Laws," *The Bankers Magazine,* CXXVI (June 1933), pp. 537-538.

30. *The New York Times,* May 19, 1933.

31. Francis H. Sissons, "How We May Have Safe Banks, The Solution Does Not Lie in the Government Guaranty of Deposits," *The Bankers Magazine,* CXXVI (June 1933), pp. 563-567.

32. *The New York Times,* May 20, 1933.

33. Ibid., May 21, 1933.

34. Aldrich to Roosevelt, May 22, 1933, President's Official File 230, Box 1, Roosevelt Papers.

35. Boston Clearing House Association to Roosevelt, May 26, 1933, ibid.

36. Fort Worth Clearing House Association to Roosevelt, May 23, 1933, ibid.

37. Missouri Bankers Association, *Proceedings of the Forty-third Annual Convention* (St. Louis, Mo., 1933), p. 43.

38. Federal Reserve Bank of New York, Executive Committee, Memorandum of Meeting, April 4, 1933, "Discussion Notes," Harrison Papers.

39. Federal Reserve Bank of New York, Board of Directors, Memorandum of Meeting, May 4, 1933, ibid.

40. Federal Reserve Bank of New York, Board of Directors, Memorandum of Meeting, June 1, 1933, ibid.

41. Steve Early to Roosevelt, March 12, 1933, President's Official File 230, Box 1, Roosevelt Papers.

42. *Business Week,* June 10, 1933, p. 8.

43. McAdoo to Roosevelt, May 10, 1933, President's Official File 230, Box 1, Roosevelt Papers.

44. *The New York Times,* June 6, 1933.

45. *Business Week,* June 17, 1933, p. 14.

46. Glass to Roosevelt, May 26, 1933, President's Personal File, Folder 687, Roosevelt Papers.

47. Roosevelt to Pierce, June 6, 1933, ibid.

48. Roosevelt to Howell, ibid.

49. *Congressional Record,* LXXVII, pp. 5768-5769.

50. Ibid.

51. Ibid., p. 5892.

52. Ibid., pp. 5863, 5898.

53. *Time,* XXI (June 26, 1933), p. 45.

54. *The Literary Digest,* CXV (June 24, 1933), p. 7.

55. A. A. Berle, *The Future of American Banking* (Lake George, N. Y., 1933), p. 7.

5 The Roosevelt Banking Policy

The bank reform legislation enacted during the first hundred days of the Roosevelt administration was neither as radical as the liberals had hoped nor as conservative as most bankers desired. It was compromise legislation designed to correct obvious defects in the federal banking laws and to afford a degree of protection to the bank depositors of the country. Both the Emergency Banking Act and the Banking Act of 1933 had as their immediate aims the restoration of the banking system to a state of normalcy. Indications were, that at a later date, the administration would again turn to bank reform.

In the period between the November election and the March banking crisis, bank reform legislation had been discussed by the Roosevelt forces. The president-elect was no stranger to the subject. As governor of the state of New York, he had been brought face to face with the problems incident to the epidemic of bank failures. Nevertheless, in New York, as in other states, bank reform legislation met with delay and postponement. Commissions were established, studies were undertaken, and recommendations were considered, but little action resulted. In his message to the legislature on January 1, 1930, Governor Roosevelt had stated: "The meshes of our banking laws have been so woven as to permit the escape of those meanest of all criminals who squander the funds of hundreds

of small depositors." He called for a revision of the entire
state banking law, and for "far more adequate inspection
facilities" for the State Banking Department.[1] The legislature took no action and in 1931 Roosevelt again asked the
Albany legislators for increased facilities to supervise and
examine banks and for approval of a measure designed to
protect thrift accounts in commercial banks. These accounts
were maintained by small depositors. Commercial banks
were not limited in their investment policies with respect
to such funds and, as a result of the numerous bank failures,
the small depositors had suffered. The governor noted that
his bill and similar bills had been actively opposed "by some
of the banking interests themselves." Commenting on the
campaign of opposition, he said:

> At the same time no plan is offered by the banking interests.
> There is only a continued prayer for delay. To my mind con-
> tinuous delay is not only unwarranted; but it is wholly against
> the public interest. If the banking interests themselves had some
> substitute plan to correct the evils and dangers which lurk in our
> banking laws, more reliance might be placed on their wisdom.
> By merely blocking all reform . . . they discredit any claim that
> their efforts are accompanied by any sincere desire to protect the
> depositors of the state.[2]

In a personal letter to his uncle, Frederic A. Delano,
Roosevelt again emphasized his reaction to the attitude of
the bankers. He wrote, "It is this apparent apathy on the
part of the bankers to a very real need which concerns me
because it results invariably in stirring up a very deep feeling
on the part of the average citizen against the small minority
which controls finances."[3]
As president of the United States, Franklin Roosevelt
would again encounter this attitude. In the first days of his
administration, he found most bankers sadly lacking in suggestions or recommendations to remedy the banking crisis.

Later, when he called upon bankers to aid in the Recovery Program, he would meet with a negative attitude. It is not unreasonable to suggest that his previous experience with bankers during his gubernatorial terms activated Roosevelt to look beyond the bankers for a solution to banking problems. He therefore sought advice from those outside the immediate field of banking. The action he finally took on bank reform, however, was orthodox.

Roosevelt met with severe criticism from the liberals and the progressives for not nationalizing the banks during the period of crisis. There seems little doubt that he could have done this, and that the bankers and the people would have accepted it. As conditions worsened, many bankers and businessmen called for just such an action. The disintegrating situation, fear of the complete collapse of the banking structure, and lack of leadership within the financial community itself all gave rise to such demands. But for the most part they were born of panic, and the business community's demand for a government bank was short-lived. With the restoration of public confidence in the American banking system, there was little evidence of continued support by banking or business interests in establishing such an institution.

Franklin Roosevelt did not believe in a government-owned and -operated bank. He believed that depositors should be protected against bad bankers, that banking should be strictly supervised, and that the ethics of banking should be maintained. In 1932, while many were urging the extension of federal control over banking, Roosevelt sent his last annual message to the New York State Legislature. In it he emphasized his conviction regarding the role of banking in a community:

We must by law maintain the principle that banks are a definite benefit to the individual community. That is why a concentration of all banking resources and all banking control in one spot or in

a few hands is contrary to a sound public policy. We want strong
and stable banks. At the same time each community must be
enabled to keep control of its own money within its own borders.[4]

The Democratic Platform of 1932 had not called for the
establishment of a govenment bank, nor had it specifically
demanded the unification of the banking system. It did advocate "a more rigid supervision of national banks" and "further restrictions of Federal Reserve Banks in permitting the
use of Federal Reserve facilities for speculative purposes."[5]
It was not at variance with the beliefs of Franklin Roosevelt;
he supported the platform without reservations or qualifications.

At Columbus, Ohio, Roosevelt made a campaign address
in which he outlined his own economic creed. He said he
believed in individualism but that he meant it "in everything
that the word implies."

> I believe that the individual should have full liberty of action to
> make the most of himself; but I do not believe that in the name
> of that sacred word a few powerful interests should be permitted
> to make industrial cannon fodder of the lives of half the population
> of the United States. I believe in the sacredness of private property,
> which means that I do not believe it should be subjected to the
> ruthless manipulations of professional gamblers in the stock markets
> and in the corporate system. I believe that the Government without
> becoming a prying bureaucracy can act as a check or counterbalance
> to this oligarchy as to secure the chance to work and the safety of
> savings to men and women, rather than safety of exploitation to the
> exploiter, safety of manipulation to the financial manipulator.

Roosevelt reaffirmed his support of a more rigid supervision
of banking and "the restriction of Federal Reserve Banks in
accordance with the original plans and earlier practices of
the Federal Reserve system."[6]

In the period that followed the election, interest centered
on the selection of the Roosevelt cabinet. Newspapers and

magazines speculated as to possible candidates for the various posts. The declining economic condition and the rapidly worsening banking situation highlighted the importance of the selection of the secretary of the Treasury. Various names were rumored to be under consideration but the general assumption was that the post would go to Senator Carter Glass of Virginia. As father of the Federal Reserve Act, sponsor of remedial banking legislation pending before Congress, former secretary of Treasury under Woodrow Wilson, and leading Democratic party expert on banking, he was the logical choice. And he became Franklin Roosevelt's choice.

The senator from Virginia and the president-elect were not strangers to one another. Both men had served in the Wilson administration. Both had been leading figures in the Democratic party during the 1920s. Carter Glass, however, had not supported Franklin Roosevelt's campaign for the Democratic nomination. He went to the Chicago convention pledged to the support of Newton D. Baker, and it was not until the final roll call that the vote of the Virginia delegation went to Roosevelt. As a loyal party man, however, Glass supported the convention's choice.

As the campaign reached its peak, the Republicans centered their attack on economic issues and warned that the Democrats, if elected, would manipulate the currency. The Democrats' Platform affirmed their espousal of a sound currency "to be preserved at all costs." Among Roosevelt's advisers were those known to have unorthodox views on monetary issues and, notwithstanding the candidate's denials, the Republican charges persisted and there was widespread speculation on the currency matter. To refute the charges the Democrats sought out Carter Glass who was known as a sound money man and was recognized for his financial acumen. Ill health had prevented the seventy-six-year old senator from actively participating in the campaign. Nevertheless, Democratic leaders urged that he speak out on

behalf of the party. Finally, when Secretary of War Patrick
Hurley charged that "should the Democratic Party succeed
at the November election the United States will be driven off
the Gold Standard," Glass could no longer remain silent and
notified Democratic national headquarters of his willingness
to speak out. Disregarding the state of his health and the
advice of his doctor, he addressed the nation by network
radio on November 2. He gave a stirring defense of Democratic policies and indicted the economic policies of the
Hoover administration.[7]

As grateful as Franklin Roosevelt was to the senator, in
offering the Treasury post to him he was motivated by political
considerations as much as by gratitude. The senator's appointment would be reassuring to the conservative southern
wing of the Democratic party and would inspire public confidence. In addition, it would have an immediate impact on
Virginia politics since it would pave the way for the appointment of Governor Harry Byrd to the vacated Senate seat.
Moreover, Glass's prestige within the Democratic party, in
Congress, and throughout the country, made the offer almost
obligatory.

Some Roosevelt supporters were dismayed at the possibility
of the appointment of a reactionary cabinet member. Former
Senator Robert Owen, who in 1913 had guided the Federal
Reserve Act through the Senate, counseled against Glass on
this basis. Owen, an early supporter of Roosevelt, wrote the
president-elect that the cabinet should "completely reflect
the opinions of those who supported you before you were
nominated, and not those who were in the move 'to stop
Roosevelt.' "[8] Roosevelt's advisers found the offer to the
Virginia senator difficult to understand. Speaking of the
selection, in retrospect, Rexford Tugwell observed that "in
spite of the political desirability of the appointment it was
hard for him to reconcile it with the President's view of the
financial situation since Glass was an 'out and out deflationist.'"

Tugwell found this selection incompatible with the president-elect's views on inflation and thought that had Glass accepted the appointment "there would have been extreme trouble."[9]

While Roosevelt's entourage found it difficult to understand the president-elect's offer, the banking community was delighted with the choice and fervently hoped the senator would accept. They feared the new administration would resort to unsound economic practices, and felt Glass would be a restraining influence who would see that the Roosevelt administration kept the primary pledge on banking and currency which Glass had written into the Democratic Platform.[10]

As the economic situation degenerated and banking problems became acute, the president-elect was further pressed to name his secretary of the Treasury quickly. President Hoover told Roosevelt that he would welcome the announcement since it would provide a focal point for communication and action on economic matters. George Harrison told William Woodin, then a director of the Federal Reserve Bank of New York and a Roosevelt supporter, that he thought Roosevelt should immediately name his secretary of the Treasury and "make a statement in effect that he was appointed to carry out the Democratic Platform regarding the balancing of the budget and maintenance of a sound currency." Woodin consulted with Roosevelt and reported to Harrison that he was sure Roosevelt would make no public statement. He thought, however, that if Glass accepted the cabinet appointment the president-elect would not object to Glass making a statement along the suggested lines. Woodin then urged Harrison to do his best to get Glass to accept. Harrison subsequently asked Admiral Cary Grayson, a close friend of Glass, to urge Glass to accept the post. Grayson told him that Roosevelt had been alerted to the importance of telling Senator Glass that he favored a balanced budget and a sound currency. The president-elect had replied that "that was in the platform and of course he was in favor of them but he could not necessarily guarantee either over a long period of time." Woodin and Harrison again discussed the appointment. Woodin asked Harrison to urge Senator Glass "to take the position without condition and rely on Mr. Roosevelt's working it out." Harrison indicated that he did not feel he could do this as he thought that Senator Glass "was right in expecting agreement on these important principles."[11]

For two months the senator debated whether to decline or accept the position. The state of his health argued against it. His doctor advised against it. Of more importance was his own growing concern over the president-elect's ambivalence on the question of inflation. In discussing the appointment with presidential adviser Raymond Moley, Glass repeatedly tried to get a firm commitment on Roosevelt's fiscal policies. Moley reported back to Roosevelt and was instructed to tell Glass "we're not going to throw ideas out of the window simply because they are labeled inflation."[12] The president-elect would make no commitment to the senator. Finally, on February 7, Glass declined the post. The offer was renewed and was declined again on February 20. In a letter to Harry Byrd, Glass wrote:

> Aside from everything else I am far from being convinced that if I retain my health I cannot be of more help to the new administration in the Senate, where God knows, it will need friends more than at the Treasury. This seems to be almost without exception the considered opinion of my colleagues on both sides of the Senate chamber.[13]

When it became known that Carter Glass had finally and absolutely declined the office of secretary of the Treasury, other names were reported to be under consideration for the post. Owen D. Young, president of General Electric and deputy chairman of the Federal Reserve Bank of New York, issued a statement declining consideration.[14] Jackson Reynolds, president of the First National Bank of New York, informed the president-elect that he was not interested in the job.[15] Huey Long, who had opposed the Glass appointment, came out in favor of Henry B. Steagall.[16] Other names were mentioned, but ultimately the appointment fell to William Woodin, the man who had so diligently urged the appointment of Carter Glass.

Woodin has been described by Rexford Tugwell as "a compromise candidate." President of the American Car and Foundry Company, William Woodin had supported the Roosevelt candidacy for the presidency, had made substantial contributions to the campaign fund, and had been an active participant in the Business Men for Roosevelt Committee. As a director of the Federal Reserve Bank of New York, he was no stranger to banking circles. A close friend of Franklin Roosevelt, he served as a trustee of the Warm Springs Foundation. Tugwell has suggested that Roosevelt turned to Woodin because he "was well-known in the banking community" and would "command confidence among bankers."[17] William Woodin was in no sense a fiscal expert, nor did he have wide experience in banking. In commenting upon the appointment, *Business Week* observed:

> Woodin is no Ogden Mills. He is, by the way, the biggest surprise of the Cabinet. Persons who pretend to be close to Roosevelt had predicted that whatever else happened Roosevelt would never go to Wall Street for his Secretary of the Treasury. But he has. Woodin is Big Business, holding all the orthodox views about sound money, guarantee of bank deposits, and a balanced budget.[18]

Time magazine described Woodin as a "'hard money' man who could be counted on to oppose all schemes for currency inflation."[19] Failing to obtain the services of Carter Glass, Franklin Roosevelt had selected for the Treasury Department post a man who was acceptable, and indeed reassur-

ing, to the conservative element in the country and to the
financial community. However, Woodin had not bound the
president-elect to pledges regarding his future action on
monetary and fiscal matters. The selection was most for-
tunate. Woodin was to serve as secretary of the Treasury
for less than one year. Although he lacked extensive
knowledge of banking and currency matters during the banking crisis, he was second only to Roosevelt as the man of the
hour. He gained the confidence of the American public and
was reassuring to American businessmen. His optimism and
buoyancy—crucially important in that somber period—were
exceeded only by that of the chief of state. His untimely
death in 1934 was mourned by the president and by the
nation.

During the banking crisis, Franklin Roosevelt did not immediately appoint other top Treasury Department personnel; for a period of time members of the Hoover administration remained on the job. Ogden Mills, outgoing secretary of the Treasury rendered immeasurable assistance to
the incoming administration. Referring to those critical
days and the men who worked together, Raymond Moley
noted that they had "forgotten to be Republicans or
Democrats . . . we were just a bunch of men trying to save
the banking system."[20] As the banking crisis passed and
conditions stabilized, new Treasury Department appointments were made. Dean Acheson was selected to fill the
post of under secretary of the Treasury. *Time* magazine
reported that the selection of this "liberal young Democrat" was expected "to offset the elderly conservatism of
his treasury chief."[21] James Francis Thaddeus [Jeffty]
O'Connor was designated comptroller of the Currency. A
onetime Los Angeles law partner of Senator McAdoo,
O'Connor had managed the Roosevelt primary in California. Essentially, this was a political appointment and
criticism was levied because of his lack of banking expe-

rience. It was reported that Senator McAdoo himself complained that O'Connor was "no banking expert."[22]

Initially, Roosevelt asked Eugene Meyer to remain as governor of the Federal Reserve Board. Meyer agreed, but no time limit was set for his stay. By the end of March, serious differences of opinion had arisen between Meyer and members of the administration over proposed Federal Reserve legislation. As a result, Meyer tendered his resignation on March 27. Roosevelt then offered the post to James Cox, presidential nominee and his running mate in the 1920 presidential campaign. Cox declined the position, stating,

> During all of my mature years my predelections, every one, have run clearly away from banking. I never bought stock in a bank, nor would I serve on a board of directors. In our whole economic set up, banking is the one thing which never inspired the least degree of interest or enthusiasm on my part. When a man is to be at the head of the institution which you want to reorganize he must find, if he is to be of service, a congenial routine. I think we can agree that there cannot be desirable results without happiness in labor.[23]

Roosevelt accepted Cox's refusal. Roosevelt's reply to Cox indicates something of his own feeling for banking:

> I do understand—fully—especially because I am like you for I have all my life, as a lawyer and businessman, run away from banking. It is the last field of human activity that appeals to me. That, however, was one of the reasons why I had so greatly hoped that you would head the Federal Reserve Board even temporarily. I do not want anyone in that job who has a passion for banking! And, also, because I know you have a superabundance of old-fashioned common sense, business acumen and with it all ideals. I felt you were highly fitted to help us put the whole financial structure on its feet.[24]

Unable to secure the services of James Cox, Roosevelt

then turned to the Federal Reserve System itself and selected Eugene Black, governor of the Federal Reserve Bank of Atlanta, to serve as head of the board. Black was a conservative with orthodox views on money and banking matters. His appointment therefore met with the approval of the banking community. In June Roosevelt completed his banking appointments by naming to the Federal Reserve Board John Jacob Thomas, a Nebraska farm-lawyer, and Matthew S. Szymczak, comptroller for the city of Chicago and friend of the late Mayor Anton Cermack. The appointment of Szymczak was criticized. Walter Lippmann commented, "It is distinctly alarming to find the President making a merely political appointment to the Federal Reserve Board."[25] Interestingly, Szymczak served on the Federal Reserve until his retirement in 1961, a period of almost 30 years.

Franklin Roosevelt's appointments in these bank-related areas served only to emphasize his conservative approach to banking. They were in close accord with the statements he had made as governor of New York and as Democratic candidate for the presidency. In retrospect, the appointments can be regarded as signposts for his future presidency: they show that the new president contemplated no immediate radical changes in the banking structure of the country.

The conquest of the banking crisis brought the administration acclaim not only from the public, but from the bankers as well. In April *The Bankers Magazine* published an editorial which called upon the bankers to "Rally Round Roosevelt": "In the face of a great emergency, the President has acted with promptness not unmixed with a proper degree of caution. He should have united support in every wise action taken with a view to rescue the country from the dire situation into which it has been allowed to drift."[26] During the spring of 1933 numerous state bankers associations held their annual conventions. Praise for the administration's action during the emergency was profuse. Bankers appeared to be reassured about Roosevelt's policies. Melvin Rouff, president of the Texas Bankers Association, said that the "emergency legislation already adopted indicates that the country is headed in the right direction. It has found the road away from disaster."[27] Francis Sissons, president of the American Bankers Association, told the Virginia bankers, meeting in convention, that while, to a certain extent" the adoption of the program was dictated by force of circumstances . . . the skill, speed and decision with which the government met the emergency brought about a reversal of public psychology which, viewed in retrospect, seemed little short of miraculous."[28]

A somewhat more realistic appraisal was given by George L. Harrison to George Seay, governor of the Federal Reserve Bank of Richmond: "It is difficult to conceive of any plan of recovery from the events of the first week in March that could be called perfect." He noted that "every proposal that was considered as a means of getting out of the difficulties in which we then found ourselves had some substantial defects. . . . "With its admitted disadvantages I am frank to confess that I do not see any that on the whole would have worked any better." Harrison felt that, even though a "terrific pressure of deflation" resulted from "the closure of so many banks, and the lockup of so many hundreds of millions of deposits . . . yet the aggregate deposits of the country as a whole, that is of all licensed banks, are probably quite adequate to take care of the present volume of the country's business." He recognized the difficulties experienced by certain localities where "there are relatively no deposits available," and said that it was "one of the worst hardships in the plan, and it ought to be attacked promptly by the reorganization of banks in those localities so as to make deposits available as soon as possible." He spoke also of the problems of nonmember state banks: "the liberal licensing of too many such institutions which

would not have passed the test applied by the Treasury
Department is a continuing threat."[29]

Throughout the emergency there was considerable concern over nonmember state banks. Prior to the emergency,
a governors' conference had been scheduled to meet with
the president on March 6 to discuss cooperation between
the federal government and the states. As a result of the
banking crisis, the president could not prepare a formal
address for the meeting. He did meet with the governors,
however, and expressed his gratitude for "what the States
have done in this emergency."

> We want if possible, to have a general banking policy, that is to
> say, one covering National banks and State banks, as uniformly
> as possible throughout the country. At the same time we want to
> co-operate with all of the States in bringing about that uniformity.
> I have no desire to have this matter centralized down here in
> Washington any more than we can help.[30]

Two days later at a press conference, a reporter, referring to
the president's statement, said, "You mentioned in your
greeting to the Governors on Monday, that you favored a
unified banking system." He asked "Is that in your emergency plan?" Roosevelt replied:

> That wasn't quite the way I put it to them, what I said to them
> was, that it was necessary to treat the State and National banks
> the same way in this emergency so there would not be two
> different classes of banks in this country; and the other thing
> I said was to try to avoid forty-eight different plans of putting
> this into effect.[31]

Roosevelt showed great concern for the fate of nonmember state banks. In his first fireside message, he promised
that they would receive assistance. This pledge was acted
upon when Senator Joseph Robinson, Democrat from Arkan-

sas, offered an amendment to the Emergency Banking Act
which provided for direct loans by Federal Reserve banks
to state banks and trust companies.[32] This measure was introduced on March 14, two days following the president's
message. The bill was opposed by the Federal Reserve Board.
Governor Meyer advised Senator Glass: "We are unanimously
of the opinion that such a law . . . would be highly inadvisable
and prejudicial to the best interests of the Federal Reserve
System and to the financial structure of the nation." Meyer
indicated that it was the board's belief that neither the system nor the country should be subjected to the hazards
involved in the proposed legislation.[33] Senator Glass was reported to have "unflinchingly opposed the bill to Roosevelt,
saying the Government had never contributed a dollar to the
Federal Reserve System." This statement, it was reported,
"surprised Roosevelt very much."[34] The president, in turn,
was said to be "strongly in favor of the measure," and was
reported to have told Meyer that "it was just a matter of administration."[35] A compromise was finally reached by limiting the availability of Federal Reserve credit to nonmember
banks to a period of one year. On March 24, the bill passed
both houses of Congress and was sent to the president, who
promptly signed it into law.[36] Designed to aid banks outside
the scope of the Federal Reserve System by utilizing Reserve
facilities and funds, this bill caused considerable concern to
the Federal Reserve authorities, and ultimately led to Eugene
Meyer's resignation from the governorship of the Federal
Reserve Board. With the passage of this bill, the harmony
that had marked the period of the banking crisis came to an
end. If, in the Emergency Banking Act, the president had
not revealed himself an advocate of a government bank, his
action in this instance showed that he was not willing to
sacrifice the state banking system to the idea of unifying
all banks under the Federal Reserve System.

Franklin Roosevelt's policies during the first hundred

days of his administration have been assessed by many historians. Two members of Roosevelt's team have made particularly perceptive observations on the banking policies followed during the period of crisis. Raymond Moley emphasized:

> The policies which vanquished the bank crisis were thoroughly
> conservative policies. The sole departure from convention lay
> in the swiftness and boldness with which they were carried out.
> Those who conceived and executed them were intent upon rally-
> ing the confidence, first of the conservative business and banking
> leaders of the country and, then, through them, of the public in
> general.

With regard to the Banking Act of 1933, Moley points out that "Roosevelt's banking policies were, in their early phase largely adaptations of Senator Glass's conservative plans for consolidation of state and national bank systems." This, together with the fact that "the Federal Reserve Board's activities were headed toward the exercise of credit control comparable to the money control F.D.R. had acquired," Moley found to be the significant facts.[37]

In his biography of Roosevelt, Rexford Tugwell emphasizes the president's pragmatic approach to the banking problem. Although "a new banking system that would take out of private hands the creation of a nation's vital medium of exchange, the setting up of deposit banks that would be merely that, and the establishment of a capital issue system with some kind of relation to national need" had all been discussed theoretically with the Brain Trust, Tugwell believes that Roosevelt found such ideas "so fantastic to those by which any system would have to be run," that "he gave up any hope of substitution." He states:

> The best Franklin could expect was that trustworthy financiers
> might be found who would carry out a liquidation of the existing

banks, getting them going again as soon as responsible management could be secured. It was obvious that confidence in resumed
operations would be hard to establish. The banks would be the same
banks, the bankers the same bankers. Some, however, would not
be allowed to reopen. There must be tests for resumption that
would prove the safety of those institutions that did resume.
When activity had been set going again and panic had been quieted,
it might be possible to achieve substantial reforms. The pressure
of the present, however, called imperatively for simple restoration
of a system people understood under conditions that would assure
them of future safety.[38]

With unwavering faith in the American system and in his
own ability to surmount the crisis, Franklin Roosevelt had
brought the nation through the bank emergency. Neither the
Emergency Banking Act nor the Banking Act of 1933 was
intrinsically related to a New Deal program. One was born
of necessity, the other of compromise. Nevertheless, the
president's control of the situation set the course for greater
government participation in banking. The development of a
Roosevelt banking program lay in the future.

NOTES

1. Daniel R. Fusfeld, *The Economic Thought of Franklin D. Roosevelt and
the Origins of the New Deal* (New York, 1945), p. 186.

2. Rosenman, *The Public Papers and Addresses of Franklin D. Roosevelt,*
I, pp. 536-537.

3. *F.D.R. Personal Letters,* III, p. 189.

4. Rosenman, *The Public Papers and Addresses of Franklin D. Roosevelt,*
I, p. 114.

5. *The New York Times,* June 30, 1932; *Congressional Record,* LXXV,
p. 14735.

6. Rosenman, *The Public Papers and Addresses of Franklin D. Roosevelt,*
I, p. 682-683.

7. Rixley Smith and Norman Beasley, *Carter Glass, A Biography* (New
York, 1939), pp. 314-319.

8. Owen to Roosevelt, January 25, 1933, President's Personal File Folder 829, Roosevelt Papers.

9. Tugwell, "Reminiscences," p. 35.

10. *Time*, XX (February 6, 1933), p. 15.

11. Harrison to Confidential Files, February 17-19, 1933, "Conversations," Harrison Papers.

12. Moley, *After Seven Years*, p. 120.

13. Glass to Byrd, February 4, 1933, Box 6. Glass Papers.

14. *The New York Times*, January 30, 1933.

15. Jackson E. Reynolds, "The Reminiscences of Jackson E. Reynolds," 168-169, Oral History Collection, Butler Library, Columbia University.

16. *The New York Times*, February 2, 1933.

17. Tugwell, "Reminiscences," pp. 35-36.

18. *Business Week*, March 8, 1933, p. 7.

19. *Time*, XX (February 27, 1933), p. 13.

20. Moley, *After Seven Years*, p. 149.

21. *Time*, XX (May 15, 1933), p. 11.

22. Ibid.

23. Cox to Roosevelt, April 4, 1933, President's Personal File Folder 53, Roosevelt Papers.

24. *F.D.R. Personal Letters*, III, p. 344.

25. Walter Lippmann, *Interpretations 1933-1935* (New York, 1936), p. 69.

26. *The Bankers Magazine*, CXXVI (April 1933), p. 310.

27. Texas Bankers Association, "Proceedings of the Forty-ninth Annual Convention," *The Texas Bankers Record*, XXII (June 1933), p. 7.

28. Virginia Bankers Association, *Proceedings of the Fortieth Annual Convention* (n.p., 1933), p. 40.

29. Harrison to Seay, April 10, 1933, "Miscellaneous Letters and Reports," Harrison Papers.

30. Franklin D. Roosevelt, *On Our Way* (New York, 1934), p. 10.

31. Rosenman, *The Public Papers and Addresses of Franklin D. Roosevelt*, II, pp. 32-33.

32. *The New York Times*, March 14, 1933.

33. Meyer to Glass, March 14, 1933, Box 5, Glass Papers.

34. "Hamlin Diary," March 15, 1933.

35. Eugene Meyer, "Reminiscences of Eugene Meyer," A130, Oral History Collection, Butler Library, Columbia University.

36. *The New York Times*, March 24, 1933.

37. Moley, *After Seven Years*, pp. 150, 193, 366.

38. Rexford Tugwell, *The Democratic Roosevelt, A Biography of Franklin D. Roosevelt* (New York, 1957), p. 264.

6

The Period of Transition July 1933- December 1934

With the passage of the Banking Act of 1933, Congress completed its work on remedial banking legislation, and on June 16, the special session adjourned. The Congress, which had met primarily to enact the president's bank emergency program, accomplished far more. In rapid succession the legislators gave the chief executive a series of major legislative measures to cope with the complex economic problems facing the nation. On March 20, the Economy Act was passed; on March 22, the Beer Act; and on March 31, the Civilian Conservation Reforestation Relief Act. On May 12, the Federal Emergency Relief Act and the Agricultural Adjustment Act were signed. On May 20, the Tennessee Valley Authority was created, and on May 27, the Securities Act of 1933 became law. On the final day of the special session, when the Banking Act of 1933 was signed, the Farm Credit Act, the Emergency Railroad Transportation Act, and the National Industrial Recovery Act also became law. In time, some of these laws would be declared unconstitutional, others would fail to achieve their aims, and a few would become landmark legislative measures. In June 1933, all provided the initial framework for the Roosevelt recovery program.

For the administration the task that lay ahead was monumental. Fear had been conquered but economic conditions had not improved substantially. Unemployment, overpro-

duction, falling prices, and credit contraction were among
the problems remaining to be solved. The banking situation
was intimately related to all of these. The immediate reopening of as many banks as quickly as possible was imperative.

Utilizing the powers granted by the Emergency Banking
Act, the Treasury Department, the Office of the Comptroller
of the Currency, the Federal Reserve System, and the state
banking authorities joined together in the tremendous task
of licensing those banks found to be sound. Banks having on
hand rediscountable assets in amounts equal to their deposits
began reopening on Monday, March 13. By March 15, banks
controlling approximately 90 percent of the banking resources of the country had resumed business on an unrestricted basis. In order that banks could meet the demands
of their depositors, the Emergency Banking Act authorized
Federal Reserve banks to issue Federal Reserve Bank notes
which could be secured by direct obligations of the United
States up to 100 percent of their value or by any notes,
drafts, and bills acquired by Federal Reserve banks up to
90 percent of value. However, throughout the country
deposits exceeded withdrawals and there was little need to
utilize the new currency provided by the emergency legislation. From California, A. P. Giannini of Bank of America
telegraphed RFC Director Jesse Jones that "the amount of
actual cash taken throughout the branches of our system on
Monday and Tuesday exceeds the cash withdrawn by one
billion, two hundred twenty-five thousand dollars. This
certainly shows that money is coming out of hoarding."[1]
Public confidence in the American banking system was
reawakening. Nevertheless, in many areas banking services
were limited and in some localities there were no banking
facilities whatsoever. Licensing of banks had been done
quickly and under great pressure. Beneath the spirit of optimism that pervaded the administration fear lurked that a
new wave of bank failures would again bring about a col-

lapse of the banking system of the country.

Prior to the enactment of the emergency banking legislation, Secretary of the Treasury Woodin requested from
the Federal Reserve banks a list of the sound banks in each
district. In New York, the Federal Reserve officials considered the task impossible. In discussing the matter, J. H.
Case, Federal Reserve agent at the New York Federal
Reserve Bank, told the executive committee of the bank's
board of directors that the Federal Reserve Board had
instructed the bank to comply with the secretary's request
"first because he [Secretary Woodin] is the chairman of
the Federal Reserve Board and second, because under the
President's proclamation he is now running the show."[2]

The officials of the New York Reserve Bank were primarily concerned over the reopening of banks on a 100-
percent basis. This provided for the full resumption of
banking operations and indicated to the public that such
banks were sound. The question of the Reserve Bank's
liability with respect to the reopening of such banks was
discussed at the director's meeting. Governor Harrison
sent word from Washington that there would be no legal
obligation upon the Federal Reserve banks with respect to
banks reopening on a 100-percent basis. Yet, he felt there
was a moral obligation. Harrison reported that he had asked
that the government guarantee the Federal Reserve banks
against loss in meeting this obligation, but that this had not
been done since the passage of such legislation at that
time was not wise. He stated that the president had written
a letter to Secretary Woodin indicating that he would ask
Congress for indemnification of the Reserve banks for
losses made on loans granted under the emergency powers.
Under these circumstances. Harrison believed that the
Reserve Bank could do nothing but accept the Treasury's
program and list those banks that could safely and reasonably
be reopened for full operations. In each case considered,

Harrison thought the Bank should bear in mind the overall program, the assurance of reimbursement against loss, and the desirability of making decisions that were neither too strict nor too liberal. The board of directors then discussed the reopening of a large group of banks in the doubtful column. L. R. Rounds, deputy governor of the New York Bank, believed that if there was any real possibility of such banks working out it would probably be wiser to let them open with the provision for internal reorganization and in hope of aid from improved external conditions. On the basis of the general banking program and the expectation of improvement in the economic situation, these banks were permitted to reopen. Throughout the country border-line cases were handled in this manner.[3]

Although federal and state officials worked diligently in examining the banks, the pressures were so great that mistakes were made. Reviewing those turbulent days, Jesse Jones recalled:

> In literally thousands of cases in those feverish days and nights it was difficult to decide whether a bank was truly sound. The plunge in values, particularly market values, made one man's guess as good or bad as another's in assessing the probable worth of many a bank's portfolio. Mistakes were inevitable. A great many unsound banks were allowed to resume business. Judged by the panic prices then prevailing, four thousand of the banks which were allowed to open after the moratorium were unsound.[4]

Despite this liberal reopening policy, numerous banks throughout the nation were in such bad financial straits that it was impossible to reopen them on more than a restricted basis. Others could not be reopened at all. By the end of May 1, 163 banks in the Federal Reserve System alone were still without licenses to do unrestricted banking business.[5] Deposits amounting to approximately $4 billion were still immobilized.[6] These, together with an even greater number of nonmember state banks, were placed under conservatorships to await reorganization or liquidation. Action on such a mass scale was unprecedented. Limited withdrawals were permitted during the period when banks were operated by conservators. Rules and instructions were of necessity involved and detailed. Delays in reorganizations were unavoidable; hardships for the banks and for the communities they served resulted. Many cities and towns were left with only restricted banking services. Bankers converged on the offices of both federal and state banking authorities. Letters indicative of the difficulties experienced flowed into Washington. Complaints and requests for aid were received by top government officials as individual bankers endeavored to gain consideration for their particular problems. A banker from upstate New York wrote to Secretary of Commerce Daniel C. Roper concerning the problems of reorganization. He asked "if it would not be possible for the Secretary of the Treasury and the Comptroller to outline a general plan on the subject." He proposed that such a plan could then be altered in individual cases, where circumstances required, whereby stockholders and depositors could make equitable and attainable contributions toward the reopening of their banks. He urged the secretary to voice "this suggestion when the subject of reopening the banks was next discussed at a cabinet meeting."[7] This request was but one of hundreds received in Washington.

To stabilize the banking situation and support the banking structure of the country, the Emergency Banking Act authorized the Reconstruction Finance Corporation to invest in the preferred stock of banking institutions. In April *The Magazine of Wall Street* suggested that the frozen assets of unlicensed banks could be converted "into at least partial liquidity without further months of delay" if more "liberal Reconstruction Finance Corporation help" were forthcoming, and indicated that such a step "would be sounder than various other schemes"

proposed to combat deflation.[8] In June Chairman Eugene
Stevens of the Federal Reserve Bank of Chicago, at the direction of his board of directors, notified President Roosevelt
that of the 2,981 banks in the seventh Federal Reserve District, 1,159 remained unopened. Of these, he said, 867 were
nonmember banks. Stevens stressed "the desirability of devising some means by which reopening of the closed banks
could be expedited."[9] That same month, *Business Week*
reported that more than 1,100 member banks and 3,900
others were still closed, and that "criticism of Administration inaction grows."[10] By August *The Commercial and Financial Chronicle* reported that 2,870 banks were either
operating on a restricted basis or had not yet been reopened,
but that the comptroller was sending special examiners to
expedite reopenings in critical areas.[11]

The administration determined to utilize fully the new
powers granted to the RFC and to establish a policy whereby
the faulty structure of the unlicensed banks could be
strengthened. The administration first proposed to encourage
people in local communities to participate in the reorganization of their local banks by investing their own money in
bank stock. It became RFC policy to purchase the preferred
stock or capital notes "of those banks whose assets appeared
to be equal to 90 per cent of their total deposits and other
liabilities exclusive of capital." This exerted pressure on the
banks' stockholders and customers to put in capital and own
their own banks.[12]

In many instances this program was successful, but by late
autumn unlicensed banks, including Federal Reserve member banks and state nonmember banks, were reported to
total more than 2,000, with combined deposits of approximately $8 billion.[13] Under the provisions of the Banking
Act of 1933, the Temporary Deposit Insurance Fund would
begin operations on January 1, 1934. Only those banks
certified as sound would qualify for insurance. In his banking

message to the nation, the president had said that all banks which reopened would be sound. Now many that had been allowed to reopen would not bear the additional inspection necessary to qualify for deposit insurance. This, added to the deflationary impact of the frozen bank funds, greatly accelerated the government's program.

However, there was resistance to too liberal a policy. Thomas J. Watson, a director of the Federal Reserve Bank of New York and president of International Business Machines, thought some banks should go out of business. He told the directors of the New York Bank that it was better to have a little crisis now rather than more serious trouble later. In discussing the matter, George Harrison observed that Senator Glass had recently expressed the same views. However, Harrison noted that at that time Washington held that all licensed banks must be put in shape for entry into the Federal Deposit Insurance Corporation. He said that the administration did not plan to negotiate with individual banks, but would have the Reconstruction Finance Corporation take the initiative and subscribe for the preferred stock of all the banks. It would be left to the individual banks to call the subscriptions. Harrison suggested that this plan would encourage the banks to issue preferred stock to the RFC. He stressed that it was the government's plan to draw the agreement so that the preferred stock issued to the RFC would be retired as soon as a bank had "restored its other capital to 10 percent of its deposits." This, he said, would enable the government to withdraw "as soon as banking effort or business conditions made that possible."[14]

In October, Roosevelt asked Henry Bruere, president of the Bowery Savings Bank, to come to Washington to assist in coordinating various activities pertaining to banking. In particular, Roosevelt told Bruere, he wanted a solution to the problem of the closed banks. To obtain a plan to deal with this problem, Bruere met with the comptroller of the Currency, the under secretary of the Treasury, the chairman of the RFC, and Carroll Merriam, a member of the RFC board. This group met as a board during the period when plans were being formulated. Bruere also sought the cooperation of the New York State superintendent of banks and invited cooperation from the clearing house groups throughout the country.[15]

Rumors were that "the President entertained the idea of forming a federal bank or special corporation with R.F.C. funds," the purpose being to liquidate all closed banks.[16] In his autobiography, Jesse Jones reveals that Bruere, together with Lewis Douglas, director of the Budget, drew up a plan to set up an organization headed by a New York banker. Jones observes that he told Bruere and Douglas "that the job would remain in the R.F.C. and that there would be no New York banker at the head of it." Jones gained the backing of the president and established a Deposit Liquidation Division within the Reconstruction Finance Corporation.

In December, as the deadline drew near for the establishment of the Temporary Deposit Insurance Corporation, administration officials feared another bank debacle if the public learned that some 2,000 banks could not qualify for coverage. To alleviate the situation, Jesse Jones conferred with Henry Morgenthau, who had replaced the fatally ill William Woodin as acting head of the Treasury Department. Jones reports:

> I told him there was a way to avoid fresh bank trouble if he would cooperate with us. I proposed that the RFC make an agreement with him which would provide that, if he would certify as solvent the banks in our hospital group [unlicensed banks], the RFC would make them solvent within six months. Mr. Morgenthau readily agreed. He really had no choice.

The agreement was put in writing and the banks were kept

open. On January 1, 1934, when the Temporary Deposit Insurance Fund began operation, all banks in the country that were open were automatically covered. They had been certified by the secretary of the Treasury as sound. The unofficial time extension allowed the RFC to strengthen the doubtful banks. In all, Jones reports that the cost to the government was $1,350,000,000.[17]

In the summer and fall of 1933, the administration sought the cooperation of the banking community to aid the recovery of business and agriculture. Banks were encouraged to participate in the Reconstruction Finance Corporation's preferred stock program so that they would be in an easy cash position to help in the work of recovery. Strong banks as well as weak banks were urged to make this move and put this additional capital to work. Most bankers, however, were reluctant to join the program. Some feared a loss of the public's confidence if it became known that their stock had been purchased by the RFC; to others the investment policy savored too much of government control of the banking system; and a third group declared there was no demand for bank credit. Even so, small industries, with depleted capital, found it difficult to obtain bank loans.

In September the annual meeting of the American Bankers Association convened in Chicago. *Time* magazine, covering the convention, reported:

> For the first time since their counting houses were all shut up and they were called "money changers in the temple" by the President of the U. S. they were assembled to consider the effect on banking of the New Deal and the national recovery program. Missionaries of Franklin Roosevelt were on hand to teach them 1, What the Administration wants, 2, to like it.[18]

The role of missionary fell to Jesse Jones. Prior to the convention, the president had instructed him to emphasize that "the government needs the willing and confident cooperation

of its banks" and "is willing to go into partnership with
them." Roosevelt told Jones to say that the banks would be
permitted to "end the partnership at will," but in the meanwhile the government would make "it easy for them to fur-
nish the credit necessary for the recovery program."[19] Jones
did not mince words. He told the bankers "to be smart for
once." He urged that they take the government into "partnership with you," and he warned that "if banks do not provide
the credit, the Government will."[20] His speech was not well
received. Bankers showed little enthusiasm for the administration's program. All the same, pressure continued and
within a few weeks a change was noted in the attitude of
some bankers. By mid-October, the Continental Illinois
National Bank and Trust Company of Chicago, the nation's
fifth largest bank, had sold to the government preferred
stock valued at $50 million.[21] By the end of the month,
nineteen large banks of the New York Clearing House Association had, as a body, promised to sell stock to the
government. It was speculated that "some rather high
powered arguments were used to drag the New York banks
into line." *Time* magazine suggested that they were perhaps
told "that the Government, if forced to, could easily enter
the banking business."[22]

In November RFC Director Jones and President Roosevelt
met with three leading New York bankers.[23] As a result of
their talks, the ice was broken and arrangements were made
for their institutions to sell preferred stock to the RFC.[24]
Following this meeting, James Perkins of the National City
Bank wrote to the president and said of the meeting: "I
never received better treatment or more intelligent cooperation than I received from Washington." He reported that the
National City Bank would sell $50 million in capital stock to
the RFC.[25] On December 5, in a letter from Perkins, shareholders of the National City Bank were advised of the contemplated action. They were assured that the president of

the United States had stated that "nothing could be further from the truth" than the fears raised in some quarters that "the Government wants to control the banks through ownership of preferred stock." Roosevelt was quoted as saying that "the Government only wants to provide banking capital adequate to meet the credit needs of the country."[26] The sale was approved by the stockholders. Other banks, in New York and elsewhere, followed suit. The banking industry was finally moving in the direction of the Roosevelt recovery program.

Opposition to deposit insurance continued throughout 1933. The American Bankers Association at its annual meeting adopted a resolution "recommending to the national Administration at Washington that it seek means for postponing the initiation of deposit insurance which under the provisions of the Banking Act of 1933, would be put in operation at the beginning of 1934."[27] Roosevelt was advised by Fred I. Kent, of the Federal Reserve Bank of New York, that "the subject most discussed at the American Bankers Association convention had to do with the guarantee of deposits." Kent wrote that "the belief that this law, if carried out might menace the whole Recovery Act was as marked among country bankers as among those in metropolitan cities."[28] The law was on the statute books, however, and regardless of his own personal feelings, Roosevelt had no intention of opposing a measure on which public opinion had been so clearly expressed.

The bankers were optimistic that when Congress reconvened some adjustment might be made in the banking legislation enacted during the first hundred days of the Roosevelt administration. The Legislative Committee of the American Bankers Association reported to its membership that "unlike the other important measures, the group of several bills which were combined and finally emerged as the Banking Act of 1933 . . . were not sent to Congress by the Adminis-

tration with a request for their passage." The report observed:
"Rather they embodied the views of their several authors and
became law largely through their insistence. . . . what is
needed most urgently now is a clarification of a number of
its sections, and announcement of the policies which will
govern the administration of various other important
provisions."[29]

In the interim between the adjournment of the special
session and the start of the new session of Congress in January
1934, the bankers had time to reflect and to assess the role
they had played during the banking crisis. They had cooperated with the government in the period of emergency.
But as a group their participation in the formulation of
emergency legislation was not significant. Faced with an
unprecedented situation, they appeared to be the most confused of all. For three years they had combatted, collectively and individually, the various banking measures considered
by the Congress, only to see them enacted into law while they
themselves stood helplessly by, condemned in the public eye
by the action of a small minority within their ranks. Their
position continued critical. Banking literature gave warning.
The Bankers Magazine in July 1933 urged: "It behooves
bankers, individually and as a profession, to take an aggres-
sive stand, to clarify the thinking of legislators and of the
public and, in not a few directions, their own understanding
of financial processes."[30] In November the same publication
carried an article stating that bankers "must strike at the
roots of our past difficulties through the formulation of a
sane legislative program for banking." The author pointed
out that this was one of the mistakes of the past. He then
noted that "bankers have consistently opposed legislative
proposals by others but failed to agree upon and submit
a constructive program of their own." He emphasized:

It is now our task to frame and execute a broad program of banking reconstruction which will include not only constructive legislation, but also plans for a voluntary house cleaning on matters outside the scope of the law. If we fail to do this, we cannot expect to regain the full confidence of the public.[31]

In the second session of the Seventy-third Congress, most legislation dealing with economic matters had an impact on banking. Administration measures, in particular those dealing with monetary management and fiscal policy, drew adverse reactions from the banking community. Legislation relating solely to bank reform was not of primary importance. Numerous bills dealing with specific banking problems were introduced and sent to committee. Some were reported out and a few passed into law. Three bills enacted during 1934 had special significance for the banking world. The first provided a one-year extension to the Temporary Deposit Insurance Fund, the second enabled the Reconstruction Finance Corporation and the Federal Reserve banks to make direct loans to industry, while the third provided for regulation of stock exchanges. The enactment of the first was undoubtedly influenced by the bankers' resistance to deposit insurance, that of the second by their unwillingness to participate more fully in the administration's credit expansion program, while the third resulted from the stock market investigations in which bankers had been so prominent.

The extension of the Temporary Deposit Insurance Fund was most directly related to commercial bank activity. It affected all commercial banks. The administration, no less than the bankers, supported the extension of the temporary plan and the postponement of permanent deposit insurance. Chairman Steagall of the House Banking and Currency Committee pressed for an increase in the amount of deposits covered. He wished to raise the insurance for individual accounts from the $2,500 as provided by the Banking Act

of 1933 to $10,000. The administration fought this move.
The president sent a message to Speaker of the House Henry
T. Rainey, requesting passage of the bill in substantially the
same form as it passed the Senate. "Personally," Roosevelt
said, "I am fairly well satisfied if we take care of ninety-seven
per cent of the depositors in this country, and the Senate
bill does this best." In a personal note to Rainey he added:

> Brother Steagall's suggestion of increasing insurance on deposits
> up to ten thousand dollars would aid only the three percent of
> rich depositors who have more than twenty-five hundred in any one
> bank. The bill as passed by the Senate takes care of the other
> ninety-seven percent who are people like you and me. Regards
> F.D.R.[32]

Despite the president's opposition, the House followed
Steagall's lead and increased the amount of coverage. The
House version also eliminated the requirement that nonmember banks which participated in the insurance fund
become members of the Federal Reserve System within two
years if they were to continue to enjoy the benefits of
deposit insurance. Governor Harrison told the executive
committee of the New York Reserve Bank that this action
might kill the bill, since the membership requirement was
"the one thing which made Senator Glass swallow deposit
insurance in the first place." Harrison noted that under the
new arrangement Glass "gets nothing he wants from the bill
in its present form and does get something to which he is
opposed."[33] When the bill was sent to conference, however,
a compromise was effected. Insurance coverage was placed
at $5,000 and compulsory Federal Reserve membership for
banks covered by the permanent deposit insurance was
postponed until July 1, 1937.

Gradually, the doctrine of deposit insurance gained acceptance by the banking community. In May 1934, *The
Bankers Magazine* commented: "Why even the bankers who

for years have denounced the insurance of bank deposits in unmeasured terms are now coming to look upon this device as something to be tolerated—even approved when limited to amount."[34] At the annual convention of the Texas Bankers Association, J.F.T. O'Connor, comptroller of the Currency, noted that "there has been a great change in the sentiment among bankers of this country with reference to the insurance of deposits. Every day evidence of this comes to my desk in Washington."[35] At the 1934 annual meeting of the American Bankers Association, the subject was again discussed. A committee report stated:

> There is no question but that the law guaranteeing deposits has reestablished the confidence of many thousands of small depositors throughout the United States. This has given a certain stability to the banking situation that might not otherwise have existed under all the conditions that have prevailed. That such confidence is not warranted does not change its effect.[36]

In the years that lay ahead, bankers were to accept the reality of deposit insurance. Their efforts centered on making the laws as equitable as possible from the banker's point of view.

As the federal government extended its activities into more and more areas of American life, the bankers voiced concern for the survival of private enterprise in banking. *The Bankers Magazine* observed: "The American banking system today faces the greatest challenge in its history. The glove has been thrown in its face in the form of deposit guaranty, and with the additional threat of Government control of banking in the offing."[37] In an editorial that same publication spoke of the socialistic tendencies of the Roosevelt administration:

> It is hardly conceivable that the tendency under consideration will go so far as to absorb the ordinary banking business of the country by the Government, or even to leave to the banks only the local business of their immediate neighborhoods. The socialization of

the banking system of the United States would be a development
of such far reaching consequences as not to be entered on without
due consideration of its consequence, not to the bankers alone,
but to the people who deal with them.[38]

The specter of a central bank continued to haunt members
of the banking community. In December 1933, Senator
Glass informed George Harrison that he did not know who
had started these proposals, unless it might be the Hearst
papers. Glass suggested that he did not think a central bank
was seriously being considered by responsible leaders in
Washington. He asserted that as long as he lived there would
be no central bank in Washington.[39] Throughout 1934 rumors persisted concerning a government takeover of the
banking field. In February James Harvey Rogers, monetary
adviser to the president, chatted informally with Governor
Harrison about the agitation for a central bank. Rogers
thought it would be impossible to have a central bank in
Washington. He felt that the only place for a central bank
was New York but "that this was impossible because of the
feeling of the rest of the country about New York." As a
result, Rogers told Harrison that he had been thinking about
"ways of making the Federal Reserve System more effective."
The two men discussed the possibility of having some of the
governors of the Federal Reserve banks serve from time to
time with the Federal Reserve Board. Rogers then suggested
that the governor of the Federal Reserve Bank of New York
be a permanent member of the board. Harrison replied that
"if he could get it through it would be one way to work it."[40]

The fires of rumor were fueled by the introduction of a
measure in the House of Representatives by T. Alan
Goldsborough, Democratic congressman from Maryland.
Goldsborough's bill called for the establishment of a Federal
Monetary Authority.[41] Monetary control rather than bank
supervision was its aim. Nevertheless, it provided for the
transfer of Federal Reserve Board powers to the proposed

central authority. Although the bill was not passed, hearings were held, and it provided an opportunity for new controversy. Throughout the summer and into the fall, speculation continued as to what move the government might make toward banking legislation. In September *Business Week* reported that "changes in the banking system loom as a big problem before the next Congress," and that the entire question of Federal Reserve requirements "may become academic if the Reserve banking system is to be superseded by a central bank." The article indicated that "the treasury's Sub-brain Trust, now studying currency and banking problems under the direction of Dr. Jacob Viner, Special Assistant to the Secretary, will report in favor of such a plan." Doubts were expressed, however, "that the President would raise the legislative storm certain to greet the introduction of a bill to abolish the Reserve System."[42] Bankers spoke out strongly against any move by the government to take over the banks. James Warburg, chairman of the Bank of Manhattan, who was a personal friend of Roosevelt's and had acted as adviser in the early days of the New Deal, spoke to a bankers group in Buffalo, New York. Warburg warned that if a system of government-owned and -operated banks was established, "we shall have passed the sentence of death upon all private business, upon all private capitalistic enterprise and upon our political, social and economic freedom." He supported the established system:

> The case against private banking . . . falls into two parts: the private banking system has failed and, therefore, Government banking is the answer. Both are wrong. Our particular kind of private banking system failed under certain circumstances. That is perfectly true. But that is quite different from saying that private banking as a whole has failed. And if private banking, as a whole had proved itself inadequate, which it has not, then it still would not follow that Government banking would be any better.[43]

In the summer of 1934, both the Treasury Department and the Federal Reserve System initiated studies on monetary and banking matters. The possibility of conflicting views was considered at a meeting of the directors of the Federal Reserve Bank of New York. The consensus of opinion was that the Treasury Department view would prevail. Owen Young pointed out that, should the Reserve System try to block something the Treasury Department wanted, it would probably not be able to do so.[44]

Cooperative action was entered upon in some areas. In August, Secretary of the Treasury Morgenthau brought together representatives from federal banking agencies that engaged in bank examinations, so that they could work out uniform policies as to examinations and requests for information. The purpose was to formulate a national bank policy.[45] For some time an Interdepartmental Loan Committee had existed, consisting of those agencies dealing with federal lending activities. They met to develop policies and coordinate activities. In the late fall, the president directed Secretary Morgenthau, chairman of the committee, to form a subcommittee to draft new banking legislation.[46]

Throughout 1934, in private and in public Roosevelt continued to reaffirm his belief in the American banking system. Early in January, when William Woodin was still secretary of the Treasury, Roosevelt told him: "It is far better to retain the federal reserve system with its comparative decentralization, together with a strong Treasury Department, than to try to create a third agency which would either become all powerful or else would amount to nothing."[47] He discussed the future of the Federal Reserve System with George Harrison and Eugene Black, the new governor of the Federal Reserve Board. He told them that "the federal reserve banks have done a good job, that they are adapted to conditions in this country," and that he wanted "to do nothing to minimize [their] powers."[48] Shortly thereafter,

Roosevelt wrote a letter to Black praising the system.

> It gives me pleasure at this time to express my appreciation of the
> splendid service that the Federal Reserve System has rendered in
> connection with our efforts to bring about recovery. . . . It has
> given firm support to the Government's effort in fighting the de-
> pression. It has stood loyally by the interest of the people by
> supplying them with a sound currency, by placing at the disposal
> of member banks a large volume of reserves available to finance
> recovery, by exerting a powerful influence toward the rehabilita-
> tion of the commercial banking structure, and by cooperating in
> every way with the government's financial program.[49]

For bankers, however, the president's words were not
quite as laudatory. In an address before the NRA Code authorities, just one year after his inauguration, Roosevelt
acknowledged a telegram sent by the American Bankers Association commemorating the event. The bankers congratulated him and expressed their "full confidence" and "sincere
desire" to cooperate in his "courageous efforts to bring about
recovery." The president told his audience "if the bankers
go along, my friends, we shall have three great elements of
American life working together: industry, agriculture, and
banking; and then we cannot stop. That telegram from the
American Bankers Association is a living illustration of the
progress we have made in that year."[50] In September, in a
radio address, Roosevelt made what many bankers considered
an invidious comparison, when, in speaking of the British
debt conversion policy, he added almost parenthetically,
"And let it be recorded that the British bankers helped."
Bankers resented the implication. *The Texas Bankers Record*
stated:

> Every person listening in to the speech caught the President's
> idea. To the man on the street it meant that the bankers were
> being slapped again, and that the banker as a class was even lower
> in respectability than before. Among the bankers themselves it

created considerable resentment. They felt that the President was
unfair in not giving credit for some very great work on the part
of the American bankers.[51]

In October the annual convention of the American Bankers Association was held in Washington, D.C. The president
agreed to address the gathering. Both the administration and
the banking leaders hoped that this occasion would strengthen
the bond between the government and the business group. In
his address the president stressed the purpose of government
and its relationship to banking. He said it should be threefold:

> First to promote the confidence of the people in banks and banking
> in view of the important service that banks and banking may perform
> for the people as a whole; second, to make this confidence a real and
> living thing by assisting banks to render themselves useful to render
> themselves worthy of this confidence through wise supervision. A
> third purpose now offers itself, and I wish with all earnestness to
> press this point tonight. Government should assert its leadership
> in encouraging not only the confidence of the people in banks, but
> the confidence of the banks in the people.

Roosevelt went on to recount the events of the past year
and a half. He indicated that he would "be only too glad to
curtail" the activities of public lending agencies "in proportion to the taking up of the slack by privately owned agencies." He said he "assumed and expected that private
business generally will be financed by the great credit
resources which the present liquidity of banks makes possible." "Our traditional system," he continued, "has been
built upon this principle, and the recovery of our economic
life should be accomplished through the assumption of this
responsibility." The president concluded that:

> It is not in the spirit of partisans, but it is in the spirit of partners
> that America has progressed. The time is ripe for an alliance of all
> forces intent upon the business of recovery. In such an alliance will

be found business and banking, agriculture and industry, and labor and capital. What an all-American team that would be! The possibilities of such a team kindle the imagination.[52]

Jackson Reynolds voiced the conciliatory views of the bankers. The association's leaders applauded the president's words. Yet, *Time* magazine recorded that, while "their big banking brothers were patching up peace with the White House," the small bankers, "the rank and filers stepped off the train fairly smoking with hatred of the New Deal and all its ways. . . . The vast majority wanted not peace but war."[53] Peace of a sort, however, had been achieved.

In the months following the bankers' convention, the New Deal banking program moved into high gear. In August Eugene Black resigned as governor of the Federal Reserve Board, and on November 11, the president appointed Marriner Eccles to the post. Eccles was a Utah banker who had come to Washington at the invitation of Henry Morgenthau and had served under Morgenthau in the Treasury Department. At Morgenthau's suggestion Roosevelt talked to Eccles about an appointment to the Reserve Board. Asked what he thought should be done with the system, Eccles drafted a memorandum outlining precise steps that could be taken to increase the power of the board and provide control over monetary matters. The appointment was announced shortly after this conference. Learning of the appointment, bankers feared that Eccles was too radical; radicals feared he was conservative. The Eccles appointment and the instructions with respect to preparation of banking legislation set the New Deal banking program on its course. The banking community would play only a small part in drafting the administration's bill. But in molding that measure into law, their impact would be far greater. Alerted to the inherent dangers of inaction, aware of the threat of government control, in the months that lay ahead, the bankers brought the force of their opinions and their united strength to the support and opposition of particular provisions of the proposed administration bill.

NOTES

1. Marquis James and Bessie R. James, *Biography of a Bank, The Story of Bank of America N.T. & S.A.* (New York, 1954), p. 373.

2. Federal Reserve Bank of New York, Executive Committee, Memorandum of Meeting, March 7, 1933, "Discussion Notes," Harrison Papers.

3. Federal Reserve Bank of New York, Board of Directors, Memorandum of Special Meeting, March 11, 1933, "Discussion Notes," ibid.

4. Jesse H. Jones, *Fifty Billion Dollars, My Thirteen Years with the R.F.C. (1932-1945)* (New York, 1951), p. 21.

5. F. A. Bradford, *Money and Banking* (New York, 1941), p. 222.

6. C. C. Chapman, *The Development of American Business and Banking Thought 1913-1936* (London, 1936), p. 212.

7. Clarence Miller, State Bank of Kenmore, N.Y., to Roper, April 19, 1933, U.S. Department of Commerce, Records of the Secretary, Record Group 40, U.S. National Archives and Record Service.

8. *The Magazine of Wall Street*, LII (April 21, 1933), p. 5.

9. Stevens to Roosevelt, June 20, 1933, President's Official File 230, Box 1, Roosevelt Papers.

10. *Business Week*, June 24, 1933, p. 23.

11. *The Commercial and Financial Chronicle*, CXXXVII (August 19, 1933), p. 1338.

12. Jesse H. Jones, *Fifty Billion Dollars*, pp. 27-28.

13. Ibid.

14. Federal Reserve Bank of New York, Board of Directors, Memorandum of Special Meeting, September 29, 1933, "Discussion Notes," Harrison Papers.

15. Henry Bruere, "Reminiscences of Henry Bruere," 153-154, Oral History Collection, Butler Library, Columbia University.

16. *Time*, XXI (October 23, 1933), p. 11.

17. Jesse H. Jones, *Fifty Billion Dollars*, pp. 27-32.

18. *Time*, XXI (September 18, 1933), p. 49.

19. Roosevelt to Jones, August 31, 1933, President's Personal File, Folder 756, Roosevelt Papers.

20. *The New York Times*, September 30, 1933.

21. *Time*, XXI (October 23, 1933), p. 49.

22. Ibid. (October 30, 1933), p. 49.

23. The bankers involved were James H. Perkins, chairman of the National

City Bank, William C. Potter, head of the Guaranty Trust Company, and Percy Johnson, president of the Chemical Bank and Trust Company. Jesse H. Jones, *Fifty Billion Dollars*, pp. 35-36.

24. Ibid.

25. Perkins to Roosevelt, November 29, 1933, President's Personal File Folder, 54, Roosevelt Papers.

26. Perkins to Shareholders of the National City Bank, December 5, 1933, ibid.

27. *The Bankers Magazine*, CXXVII (October 1933), p. 389.

28. Kent to Roosevelt, September 12, 1933, President's Personal File, Folder 744, Roosevelt Papers.

29. American Bankers Association, *Reports of the Fifty-ninth Annual Convention* (Chicago, Ill., 1933), p. 8.

30. R. A. Heflebower, "Should Banks Take the Blame," *The Bankers Magazine* CXXVII (July 1933), p. 18.

31. George V. McLaughlin, "A Legislative Program for Banking, The Need for Revision of the Glass Steagall Act," *The Bankers Magazine*, CXXVII (November 1933), p. 495.

32. *F.D.R. Personal Letters*, III, p. 395.

33. Federal Reserve Bank of New York, Executive Committee, Memorandum of Meeting, May 28, 1934, "Discussion Notes," Harrison Papers.

34. *The Bankers Magazine*, CXXVIII (May 1934), p. 477.

35. Texas Bankers Association, "Proceedings of 50th Annual Convention," *The Texas Bankers Record*, XXVI (June 1934), p. 42.

36. American Bankers Association, *Reports of the Sixtieth Annual Convention* (n.p., 1934), p. 42.

37. R. E. Doan, "A Challenge to Bankers," *The Bankers Magazine*, CXXVIII (April, 1934), pp. 369-370.

38. *The Bankers Magazine*, CXXVIII (March 1934), p. 250.

39. Federal Reserve Bank of New York, Board of Directors, Memorandum of Meeting, December 7, 1933, "Discussion Notes," Harrison Papers.

40. Ibid., February 15, 1934.

41. *Congressional Record*, LXXVII, p. 1037.

42. *Business Week*, September 1, 1934, pp. 28-29.

43. *Time*, XXIII (September 24, 1934), p. 574.

44. Federal Reserve Bank of New York, Board of Directors, Memorandum of Meeting, June 14, 1934, "Discussion Notes," Harrison Papers.

45. Henry Morgenthau, Jr., "Diaries," August 1, 1934, Morgenthau Papers, Franklin D. Roosevelt Library. (Hereafter referred to as "Morgenthau Diaries.")

46. John M. Blum, *From the Morgenthau Diaries, Years of Crisis 1928-1938* (Boston, 1959), p. 344.

47. Roosevelt to Woodin, January 22, 1934, President's Personal File, Folder 258, Roosevelt Papers.

48. Federal Reserve Bank of New York, Board of Directors, Memorandum of Meeting, February 1, 1934, "Discussion Notes," Harrison Papers.

49. Roosevelt to Black, February 10, 1934, "Miscellaneous Letters and Reports," ibid.

50. Rosenman, *The Public Papers and Addresses of Franklin D. Roosevelt,* III, p. 131.

51. *The Texas Bankers Record,* XXVI (October 1934), p. 33.

52. Rosenman, *The Public Papers and Addresses of Franklin D. Roosevelt,* III, pp. 435-440.

53. *Time,* XXII (November 5, 1934), p. 55.

7

A New Deal Banking Bill: The Banking Act of 1935

The Banking Act of 1935, the end product of the combined efforts of the federal banking agencies, was in all respects an administration bill. Drafted by the president's order, the provisions welded together by his design, the contents cleared by his approval, and the law brought to fruition by his intercession, it can be considered as nothing less than a Roosevelt measure. However, on February 4, when the president sent copies of the bill to the respective chairmen of the Senate and House Banking and Currency Committees, no formal message accompanied the legislation. The president merely indicated that the bill was a tentative measure prepared by Governor Eccles of the Federal Reserve Board, Chairman Crowley of the Federal Deposit Insurance Corporation, and Comptroller of the Currency O'Connor. He pointed out that he would be glad to have these gentlemen testify before the committees if it was so desired.

On February 5, the bill was introduced in the House of Representatives by Chairman Steagall,[1] and on the following day it was introduced in the Senate by Chairman Fletcher.[2] There was an immediate reaction to the new banking proposals. In its proposal of radical changes in the Federal Reserve System, the measure encountered tremendous opposition from the banking community and from Senator Glass. The fight for its passage was to be hard and

bitter. Its course through Congress witnessed a disintegra-
tion of the united front presented by those who originally
drafted the measure and a threat of dismemberment of its
omnibus whole into separate bills. Only in the final days
of the session would passage be achieved. Yet, when enacted,
the Banking Act of 1935 marked an administration victory
in the direction of monetary management, credit control,
and federal supervision of banking.

Throughout 1934, while the banking community and
the press speculated on the possibility of additional New
Deal bank reforms, the administration remained silent. It
was not until the fall that Roosevelt turned his attention
to the subject. On November 26, Secretary Morgenthau,
acting under the president's instructions, told his Interdepartmental Loan Committee that a subcommittee would
be established to act as a clearing house for banking legislation to be introduced in the coming Congress, and suggested that "it would be wise to have a meeting of the
minds before bills were presented." He asked each agency
to agree upon the legislation it desired and to report back
to the committee in two weeks. He informed the committee
that "one omnibus bill" was "the desire of the President."

Immediate opposition emerged. Chairman Crowley of the
Federal Deposit Insurance Corporation pressed for the early
advancement of legislation dealing with his agency. He
proposed that only a minimum of legislation be requested
at the coming Congress, "on the theory that legislation for
the FDIC is necessary, and the greater the added burden on
their requests the greater the difficulty in securing enactment." Others supported the president's plan. Chairman
Jones of the RFC and Chairman Eccles of the Federal Reserve
Board held that "if there is legislation the agencies want and
the President want they would get it through better now
than later." After considerable debate, it was agreed that the
individual agencies would draft recommendations which

would be reported back to the subcommittee, where they would be molded into one omnibus banking bill. It was further agreed that no publicity would be given to the work of the subcommittee other than a "statement that the members had met and discussed problems."[3]

Subsequent meetings were held in the weeks that followed. Separate sessions were devoted to discussing the recommendations of each of the federal banking agencies. on December 10 federal deposit insurance legislation was considered, on December 19 recommendations of the Federal Reserve Board were made, and on December 28 legislative proposals relating to national banks were presented. Representatives of other federal agencies attended the proceedings and participated in the discussions whenever banking legislation overlapped their areas of interest.

A number of the amendments proposed by the Office of the Comptroller of the Currency and the Federal Deposit Insurance Corporation were of a technical nature designed to clarify existing laws and correct obvious defects. Many of these had been introduced in the previous session of Congress where they had been incorporated into one omnibus measure. This measure was sidetracked during the final rush of business of the session. Reactivated, these amendments now caused little controversy.[4]

Other recommendations made by these agencies were of far greater importance. Both Comptroller O'Connor and Chairman Crowley urged their immediate consideration, and felt they should have priority over other banking legislation. Two items were of prime importance. On July 1, 1935, the permanent deposit insurance fund would begin operations. Recommendations were made to ease the nature and rate of the FDIC assessments on insured banks. Bankers supported this amendment since its enactment would grant relief to their institutions. The enactment of these provisions would lessen banker resistance to deposit insurance. Relief with respect to a July 1 deadline was also of importance to the comptroller of the Currency. Under the provisions of the Banking Act of 1933, executive officers of national banks were required to divest themselves of any loans granted to them by their own institution by July 1 or to forfeit their jobs. The comptroller proposed to amend the law and grant a time extension. Since many bankers had not complied with the law the time extension was greatly desired. The comptroller held that this amendment should have early priority and that its recommendation should be incorporated in his annual report that would be submitted to Congress prior to the introduction of any omnibus banking bill.[5] Discussed in detail, the recommendations of the Federal Deposit Insurance Corporation and the Office of the Comptroller of the Currency were considered and approved. However, both Comptroller O'Connor and Chairman Crowley, who were prevailed upon to comply with the expressed desire of the president, agreed that these proposals should be incorporated in the omnibus measure.

When Marriner Eccles accepted the governorship of the Federal Reserve Board, he did so with the understanding that he would be allowed to initiate a legislative program that would drastically alter the Federal Reserve System. Prior to his appointment, he prepared a memorandum for the president proposing what he considered desirable changes in the system. Eccles believed in the "conscious control and management of the supply of money," that it could be used "as an instrument for the promotion of business stability." In this connection he felt that "two important duties devolved upon reserve administration." The first, he indicated, was to assure "that recovery does not result in an undesirable inflation,"and the second was to assure "that a recovery was not followed by a depression." To achieve these goals he recommended two major changes in the administration of the Federal Reserve System:

1. Complete control over the timing, character and volume of open
   market purchases and sales of bills and securities by the Reserve
   Banks should be conferred upon the Federal Reserve Board.
2. The Governors of the individual Federal Reserve Banks should
   be appointed annually by their Board of Directors subject to the
   approval of the Federal Reserve Board.

Eccles considered such changes essential because they provided an increase in the authority of the Federal Reserve
Board and thus gave some prospect of success in rendering
"prompt support for emergency financing in case of need,"
and in preventing both "the recovery getting out of hand"
and the "recurrence of disastrous depressions in the future."
Eccles argued for the necessity of strengthening the authority
of the Federal Reserve Board. He said, "it is generally con-
ceded that in the past it has not played an effective role, and
that the system has generally been dominated by the Governors of the Federal Reserve Banks." He attributed "the
relatively minor role played by the Board" to "its lack of
authority to initiate open market policy, and to the complete independence of the Reserve Bank Governors." Eccles
added that "far and away the most important instrument
of reserve policy is the power to buy and sell securities in
the open market." Noting that under the present organization the "Board possessed only the power to approve or
disapprove" open market operations, he pointed out that
"the effective power over money rests with the individual
reserve banks and not with the Board." In addition, he said
that the governors "have positions of major importance in
influencing policy." He believed that "if the power of approval
of the appointments of the Reserve Bank governors were conferred on the board, the possibility of lack of cooperation
and friction would be obviated in the future while the prestige of the board would be enhanced. He drew attention to
the agitation for central banking:

The adoption of these suggestions would introduce certain attributes of a real central bank capable of energetic and positive action without calling for a drastic revision of the whole Federal Reserve Act. Private ownership and local autonomy are preserved but on really important questions of policy, authority and responsibility are concentrated in the Board. Thus effective control is obtained while the intense opposition and criticism that greets every central bank proposal is largely avoided.[6]

Eccles discussed these proposals with the president. Roosevelt, backed by the results of the recent congressional elections, was intent upon a large-scale government spending program, the financing of which would entail the cooperation of the Federal Reserve. A reorganized system would greatly facilitate this program. At the conclusion of their talk, the president remarked, "Marriner, that's quite an action program you want. It will be a knock-down and drag-out fight to get it through. But we might as well undertake it now as at any other time. It seems to be necessary."[7]

Upon taking office as governor of the Federal Reserve Board, Eccles informed the other members of the board that a new legislative program would be drafted. With board approval he discharged the System Committee on Legislation established by his predecessor, Eugene Black. Eccles felt that that committee, which was chaired by George Harrison and had only one Federal Reserve Board representative, represented the viewpoint of private bankers rather than that of the board. He informed Harrison that "from the point of view of the Board's responsibility and my own intentions—to have a Legislative Committee controlled in any way by the officers and directors of the Federal Reserve banks" was "doubly incompatible." At Eccles' suggestion the board designated a new committee composed of Federal Reserve Board personnel. It was this committee that was to do "yeoman work on the Banking Act of 1935."[8]

When the Interdepartmental Subcommittee on Banking

Legislation met to discuss proposals on the Federal Reserve
System, Eccles presented the program which he had previously discussed with the president. He made additional
recommendations to streamline the system as a whole and
to change the composition of the board itself. Discussion
centered on the powers of the Federal Reserve Board, the
changes affecting the Open Market Committee, and the
role of the Federal Reserve banks. Secretary Morgenthau
emphasized that "the two things which he, the President
and Mr. Eccles had agreed upon some weeks ago were that
the Federal Reserve Board be given veto power over appointments of the Governors of the Federal Reserve banks and
that the Open Market Committee should be appointed and
controlled by the Federal Reserve Board." Morgenthau said
he stood on that and would work for it, but he "could not
guarantee anything more than that."[9]

On January 17, 1935, when the Subcommittee on Banking Legislation met with the president, the legislative program was still unresolved. Recommendations proposed by
the FDIC and by the Office of the Comptroller of the
Currency were discussed. With regard to the Federal Deposit
Insurance Corporation proposals, the president thought "the
bill could be passed." He was concerned, however, "about a
multiplicity of bills" and insisted that the recommendations
made by the FDIC and the comptroller be combined in one
bill.[10] Later, the president met with Secretary Morgenthau
and Governor Eccles and discussed Federal Reserve legislation. By January 30, the subcommittee had drafted an
omnibus banking bill. Chairman Crowley and Comptroller
O'Connor continued to express a preference for separate
bills, but the subcommittee adhered to the president's
wishes and consolidated all approved recommendations into
one measure composed of three titles.[11]

The design of the bill was not by chance. Eccles has written that the strategy consisted in "tying something the

bankers didn't want to something they wanted very much.'"[12]
Title I pertained to the Federal Deposit Insurance Corporation. Among desired items, it proposed to change the existing law so that the rate and nature of FDIC assessment
would be liberalized to the advantage of the banking community. Title II dealt with the proposed changes in the
Federal Reserve System, and Title III contained the desired
proposal granting relief to those executive officers of banks
who were required to liquidate their loans prior to July 1, 1935.
Realizing that the full impact of the opposition would be
directed against the second section of the bill, the administration by intent so constructed the measure as to protect
the most controversial title of the bill.

The Interdepartmental Subcommittee on Banking Legislation met again on February 4. Chairman Crowley of the
FDIC and Comptroller of the Curency O'Connor reported
that Senator Glass had requested and had been given a copy
of the legislation pertaining to deposit insurance. Marriner
Eccles objected to this action. He stated that the senator had
also asked to see the Federal Reserve proposals but he had
told him that they were not in final form and that he did
not think Glass would be interested in mere proposals.
Crowley and O'Connor pointed out that the FDIC legislation
had been ready for weeks, and that they felt "it was desirable,
perhaps necessary to give it to him and that this had been
done." The subcommittee then learned that Henry Steagall,
chairman of the House Banking and Currency Committee,
feared that Glass would introduce the FDIC bill that day and
was asking for the same privilege. When he realized that the
release of the new banking proposals could precipitate a
crisis, Secretary Morgenthau immediately contacted the White
House. The president advised the secretary that he would
speak to Steagall by phone at 2 P.M. if Steagall would wait
that long. Steagall agreed to do so. The subcommittee
promptly gave final clearance to the onmibus banking bill.

The bill was immediately sent to the White House on the theory that "if the bill was cleared with the President by 2 p.m. Congressman Steagall and Senator Fletcher would be permitted to introduce all three titles." This, the subcommittee felt, "would make it appear that Steagall was working with the President, and he would be at no disadvantage" should Senator Glass introduce one title of the bill.[13] Chairman Steagall agreed, no bill was introduced by Senator Glass, and the way was cleared for the presentation of the administration's omnibus banking bill.

With the introduction of the bill in both the House and the Senate, the provisions of the Banking Act of 1935 were made public. Reaction was spontaneous. As expected, the brunt of the opposition was directed against Title II. On February 6, *The Journal of Commerce* stated "opposition to the further transfer of control over credit policies from the direction of the regional banks to the Reserve Board is general."[14] A *Wall Street Journal* editorial reported that "as a whole the bill has been ingeniously drawn to set up the substance of a central bank, virtually though not technically as subdued to the will of the Administration as if the central reserve bank was legally the property of the government."[15] *Business Week* announced that the "Federal Reserve Board proposed to take over the System lock, stock and barrel," but that the bankers were not alarmed because "a privately owned system for all the government domination, is preferable to an outright central bank."[16]

The House of Representatives moved quickly to consider the bill. On February 21, hearings were initiated by the full Banking and Currency Committee under the chairmanship of Henry B. Steagall. Chairman Crowley, Comptroller O'Connor, and Governor Eccles were requested to appear before the committee. The leadoff witness was Crowley, who spoke in support of Title I dealing with the Federal Deposit Insurance Corporation. O'Connor appeared on behalf of Title III, which included the technical amendments to the National Bank Act. The most extensive testimony by far was that of Marriner Eccles in defense of Title II containing the proposed changes in the Federal Reserve System. For ten days Eccles appeared before the committee to answer probing and exacting questions and to explain in detail the amendments to the Federal Reserve Act and the rationale behind the proposals. In the course of his testimony Eccles offered the committee eight modifications to the Banking Act of 1935 as introduced. In part, these modifications departed from the agreement arrived at by the administration's Subcommittee on Banking Legislation which drafted the original bill. One amendment in particular—an amendment dealing with the composition of the Open Market Committee—was to cause additional dissension among the original drafters of the bill.

The House hearings lasted for twenty-five days. Representatives from the administration testified for a total of eighteen days. On the remaining seven days, seventeen additional witnesses representing banking, business and agricultural interests, monetary theories and professional economics appeared. Most favored the bill, some vehemently opposed it, while others advocated additional amendments and revisions. A statement of recommendations of a special committee of the American Bankers Association was presented by their general counsel. It stated in part:

> While the committee realize that certain provisions of Title I of the pending bill affect adversely the larger banks, and that other provisions of the bill are not entirely acceptable to some of the (Federal Reserve) nonmember banks, they believe that the aims and purposes expressed in the provisions of Titles I and III of the bill are, in the main, in the public interest of banking. The committee have therefore, on behalf of the Association approved in substance titles I and III of the bill.

With respect to Title II, the committee held that certain

"constructive changes should be made." Specific suggested changes were of a moderate nature. The association called for the "absolute independence of the Federal Reserve Board from partisan or political considerations," and held that governors of the Federal Reserve banks should hold office for at least three years. The association also expressed dissatisfaction with a five-man Federal Open Market Committee and suggested that the composition should consist of the entire Federal Reserve Board and four governors of the Federal Reserve banks. Other suggestions were that the Reserve Bank governors on the Open Market Committee should be selected annually by all the governors of the Reserve banks; that "serious consideration should be given to the desirability of fixing limits in percentage of deposits beyond which reserve requirements cannot be increased or decreased by action of the open market committee"; and that the provisions permitting advances against real estate should be modified. The statement indicated that "if changes substantially along these lines cannot be made in the original draft of the bill, we would be strongly opposed to the enactment of title II."[17]

The House hearings were concluded on April 9. The hearings were top-heavy with witnesses expressing the administration's views. Apart from the testimony on behalf of the American Bankers Association, banking views were represented by a scattering of bankers identified primarily with small banks. No New York bankers testified, and no testimony was solicited from the regional Federal Reserve banks.

Because of testimony which primarily reflected Eccles' recommendations, Chairman Steagall introduced a revised banking bill in the House of Representatives.[18] Two changes were of particular importance. One placed the open market operations directly in the hands of the Federal Reserve Board rather than in an Open Market Committee dominated by board members, and the other provided the board

with a mandate which explicitly stated that the board
was required "to exercise such powers as it possesses in
such manner as to promote conditions conducive to business
stability and to mitigate by its influence unstabilizing fluc-
tuations in the general level of production, trade, prices, and
employment so far as may be possible within the scope of
monetary action and credit administration."[19] The revised
bill was approved and reported out of the House Banking and
Currency Committee on April 19. As a result of the Eccles
recommendations, the intent of the original bill was
strengthened with respect to the centralization of control in
the Federal Reserve Board. In addition, the bill provided for
the elimination of the requirement that nonmember state
banks become members of the Federal Reserve System after
July 1, 1937, as a prerequisite for membership in the FDIC.
This action was consistent with the House of Representatives'
earlier views and with Steagall's support of the state banking
systems. The bill as reported went to the floor of the House
where it was debated. No major changes were made in the
course of the debate and on May 9, 1935, the Banking Act
of 1935 passed the House of Representatives.[20] Action by
the Senate continued to be delayed.

   While the House considered the banking bill and the
Senate continued to delay action, the financial press intensified its attack upon the administration's proposal. Bankers
were taken to task for not offering more vigorous opposition
to the banking legislation. *The Commercial and Financial
Chronicle* stated, "We fear that our leading bankers have
for the most part not yet fully realized what the implications
and probable consequences are, or are likely to be." *The
Chronicle* found it "impossible to believe that bankers of
foresight and understanding could be complacent before a
proposal to grant the politicians the authority to change the
reserve required of them at will and without limit."[21]
Business Week editorialized that:

The Administration is about to achieve economic dictatorship in this country by the simple procedure of confiscating complete control of our banking and credit structure. Neither organized business nor organized banking has done anything to prevent this seizure. In fact they have not even protested. This on the theory that any protest of theirs might goad the Administration into more drastic schemes of confiscation and socialization, although just what could be more drastic than the implied ramifications of the present move is difficult to conceive.[22]

The American Bankers Association was criticized for not taking a stronger stand against the bill. *Business Week* reported that "the ABA would trade centralized control over 40 billion of banking resources for removal of government members of the Federal Reserve Board."[23] *The Texas Bankers Record* stated:

State banks all over the nation—particularly the country banks—have charged that the A.B.A. committee in agreeing "in general" to Title I of the Banking Act now before Congress "sold them out." They objected particularly to compulsory membership in the Federal Reserve System after 1937, in order to enjoy FDIC membership.[24]

The Commercial and Financial Chronicle expressed its "disappointment with the stand taken by the American Bankers Association," reporting that "the spokesmen for the Association appear to realize the far reaching implications of what is proposed, but apparently they do not fully grasp the hazards involved or else they are beset with a feeling of futility in opposing the Administration."[25]

While members of the banking community found opposition futile, officials of the Federal Reserve banks were placed in a much more difficult position. No representatives of the Federal Reserve banks appeared before the House Banking and Currency Committee to offer testimony on the proposed banking legislation. No advance notice was given to the Reserve banks with respect to the provisions of the bill. On February 7, after the provisions had been made public, the bill was discussed at the directors' meeting of the Federal Reserve Bank of New York. George Harrison, reporting on the background of the bill, discussed Eccles' role in drafting the legislation. He was concerned about what he considered to be the "star chamber procedures" adopted in devising the measure, and felt that they indicated that the administration intended to use the Federal Reserve System as a tool to advance its own program. Harrison pointed out that the Reserve banks would have an opportunity to testify before the Senate committee and felt it would be "a muddy affair" because of the way the bill was drafted and introduced. Four days later the banking bill was considered by the executive committee of the board of directors. Harrison reviewed the measure and pointed out that certain provisions placed a large measure of credit control in the Federal Reserve Board, and, in turn, in the hands of the administration. He felt those provisions should be revised. Owen D. Young contended, however, that as long as stockholding member banks had theoretical power to control the Federal Reserve banks there was little chance that they would retain credit powers in the Federal Reserve banks. Should this situation be changed, Young believed, it would considerably lessen the argument for concentration of power in Washington. Harrison agreed with this assessment.[26] Discussion then turned to the question of the appointment of the governor of the Federal Reserve Board. The executive committee determined that for the time being the best policy would be to try to preserve some independence for the Federal Reserve banks, and not to endanger this stand by taking a position on the appointment of the governor of the Federal Reserve Board.[27]

Although the administration's banking bill had been introduced in the Senate on February 6, hearings on the bill

were not held until April 19. The bill was first sent to the
Senate Banking and Currency Committee. The administration hoped that the measure would be considered by the
full committee, but this was not to be. By unanimous vote
of the committee, the bill was handed over to the Subcommittee on Monetary Policy, Banking, and Deposit Insurance
chaired by Carter Glass. Two factors contributed to the
delay in the hearings. Five members of the subcommittee
were members of the Appropriations Committee which was
also chaired by Senator Glass. In February the senator
stated that "intense hearings" would be held on the banking
bill, but that "moves in that direction would be postponed
until the Senate had passed the Relief Bill," a major administration measure then under consideration by the Appropriations Committee.[28]

Marriner Eccles' appointment to the Federal Reserve
Board was a recess appointment subject to confirmation by
the Senate. In the interim, pending consideration of the
banking bill, the Glass subcommittee turned its attention to
the Eccles confirmation. Whether by accident or intent,
Franklin Roosevelt had not consulted with Senator Glass
prior to the Eccles appointment. As father of the Federal
Reserve Act and leading exponent on banking matters, Glass
keenly resented this oversight. Furthermore, during the
formulation of the administration's banking bill, Glass was
not made privy to the reforms proposed for the Federal
Reserve System. Many of the proposed changes were completely against his conservative thinking. As a result, he
actively opposed Title II of the banking bill. To one correspondent he wrote: "The Eccles bank plan is opposed to the
whole history and tradition of the Democratic Party, and it
is something never attempted to be done by even a central
bank of Europe."[29] To another he said: "it is a dangerous
bill by a dangerous man."[30] To his friend H. Parker Willis,
who had helped draft the original Federal Reserve Act, the

senator stated: "I am not yet rid of the five billion dollar
Appropriation Bill and as soon as that is out of the way, I
must go on the Eccles Banking Bill and do my best to wreck
it. I have some hope also of wrecking Eccles."[31] Glass tried
to persuade the subcommittee to vote against confirmation
of the Eccles appointment. The vote was a close 4 to 3 in
favor of confirmation.[32] When the final vote was taken by
the full Senate, Carter Glass was again defeated: the senator
cast the only opposing vote on Eccles' confirmation.[33]

The pending appropriations legislation and the hearings on
the Eccles confirmation delayed the Senate Banking and
Currency Subcommittee's consideration of the remedial banking bill. Hearings did not begin until April 19; they continued
through June 3. More than sixty witnesses testified. Banking
interests were well represented. Senator Glass had consulted
with members of the banking community regarding possible
witnesses. He had asked George Harrison for suggestions, and
in turn Harrison reported that he had contacted other Federal Reserve banks in an effort to get suggestions for possible
witnesses from districts outside New York.[34] On a purely
personal basis, the governor furnished Glass with a technical
summary of the provisions of Title II, together with an
analytical memorandum which discussed some of the effects
of the proposed bill together with the "philosophy evidently
behind some of its provisions." Harrison told the senator that
"there are many of the provisions of Title II which we feel
would be helpful and in the interest of better administration
of the Reserve System." He noted that while some departed
from the original concepts of the Federal Reserve System,
"some of these departures we feel justified in the light of
changed conditions." Others he believed "to be fraught with
unnecessary risks and danger." Harrison told Glass that
personally he would have deferred any fundamental banking
legislation, but

The difficulty with postponements is that already there has been so much discussion of the proposed bill and so many movements for legislation affecting the Federal Reserve System, that I doubt now whether it is possible entirely to defer consideration of Title II. That being so, there remains the practical question of what modifications can properly be supported with a view to meeting the program of the Administration and the attacks of various other groups, without in any way sacrificing valuable principles of central banking.

Harrison called for the preservation of the "independent status of the Board's Governor"; for the preservation of the "regional system" and the independence of the Reserve Bank governors; and for "adequate representation in the councils of the system" for the Federal Reserve banks.[35]

When the hearings began, members of the banking community emphasized these views again and again. The testimony of the first witness, James P. Warburg of the Bank of Manhattan, set the theme for much of what was to follow.

Let me state at the outset that I am unequivocally opposed to the present enactment of Title II of the proposed bill, with or without modifications. I say this for three reasons: (1) Because I am convinced that no amount of changes which might be made in this section of the bill would in any way alter its fundamental purpose or materially alter the practical results of its enactment; (2) because I profoundly disagree with the fundamental purpose of this section of the bill; and (3) because there is no present emergency which necessitates hasty action, whereas there is every reason why a matter of such far reaching effect upon the future economic welfare of the country should be given the most careful study by competent authorities.[36]

Warburg's views were reiterated by the bankers who came before the subcommittee. Frank C. Ferguson, president of the Hudson County National Bank of Jersey City, told the subcommittee, "Our money and banking mechanism should be the outgrowth of a careful, deliberate and impartial study and analysis of our money and banking problems should be conducted by our most competent experts."[37] Indicating that the bill was more than a banking bill, that it was a credit and currency bill, Winthrop Aldrich of the Chase National Bank testified that "this is not liberalizing the Federal Reserve System. It is making it over into an instrument of despotic authority." He noted the subordination of the banks to the Federal Reserve Board and spoke of the political control inherent in the measure. Regarding the Open Market Committee, he said that "it appears that the objective of the bill is to put into the hands of a few people . . . the power to manipulate the credit and currency system of the United States in furtherance of a plan or a sequence of plans, which they themselves may draw up."[38] James H. Perkins, chairman of the National City Bank, urged "postponement of this title until the best qualified minds of the country can explore the whole subject of our banking system in the hope that a new law may be enacted which will stand the test for at least a quarter of a century." He said that he had "a great deal of skepticism that this idea of the centralization of control and responsibility will work as well in practice as it sounds in theory," and that "Title II fundamentally changes our banking system. It places in the hands of a board the power to dictate arbitrarily the money policies of the country."[39]

The arguments presented to the subcommittee were repeated in the literature published by banking interests. *The Girard Letter*, published by the Girard Trust Company of Philadelphia, stated: "Title II of the Administration's proposed Banking Act of 1935, although it does not provide for a governmentally owned central bank—if enacted would complete the government's control over the Federal Reserve System; and would make it for all practical purposes as subservient to the whims of political influence as if it were actually owned by the government."[40] In May *The Bankers*

Magazine noted "the growing demand for a banking and currency commission," and indicated that it "arises from the conviction that delay in legislation is preferable to hasty and ill considered action."[41]

The testimony given before the Senate subcommittee and the editorializing that took place in banking literature were augmented by propaganda directed to bank stockholders and depositors. In May a letter signed by William C. Potter, chairman of the board of the Guaranty Trust Company of New York, was sent to the stockholders of that institution. It stated that the provisions of the Banking Act of 1935 were "fundamentally at variance with the original conception of the function of our Federal Reserve system and of central banking in general, and it is our belief that if the measure should be enacted in its present form, the consequences would run through the entire economic fabric of the nation." The letter also took issue with the general principle of deposit insurance as embodied in Title I of the bill, but contended that the proposal was less objectionable than that included in the Banking Act of 1933. The major protest was lodged against political control of the Federal Reserve System.

> We maintain that the changes proposed in this banking bill are of such fundamental importance that they should be given the most careful and deliberate consideration before action is taken. All points of view should be examined and sifted. This could best be done by a non-partisan and in part non-political group qualified by experience and background to undertake a thorough investigation of the entire subject of banking and credit.[42]

The Guaranty Trust Company letter was followed by a similar communiqué to the depositors, trust customers, and stockholders of the Bankers Trust Company of New York City. This letter denounced Title II, stating that it "cannot cure the major defects in our banking system. It does not even recognize them. No plan of politically managed credit

control can take the place of sound credit policies. . . . Unless
we are willing to set up a banking structure and devise a
system of supervision which will prevent the kind of banking
that led to our recent difficulties, there is no way we can
avoid the consequences." The letter concluded with the
recommendation "that the passage of Title II should be
postponed and that further consideration be given to the
questions involved."[43] Other institutions took comparable
steps. The president of the Merchants National Bank of
Boston told his depositors and stockholders, "No emergency has been shown requiring the passage of Title II and
it should not pass." He urged the depositors and stockholders to "communicate your views to the Senate Committee on Banking and Currency or to the Senators representing
your state."[44] In response to this move, *The Literary Digest*
commented: "All at once and with accord that suggests timing,
they have shelved all pretense of amity with the Administration and have appeared in the open, coats off, to fight the
banking bill to the end."[45]

As congressional hearings continued, bankers and business
groups alerted their memberships to the dangers they believed to be inherent in the Banking Act of 1935. Rudolph
Hecht, president of the American Bankers Association, told
the members of the Senate subcommittee that copies of the
March "recommendations of the Association had been mailed
to the 12,000 members with a covering letter urging a careful
reading and earnest consideration of the statement setting
forth the position of the Association."[46] The Association of
Reserve City Bankers urged an independent study and
"thought it desirable to get the cooperation of other banking
associations." At their annual convention it was reported that
the American Bankers Association, the Investment Bankers
Association, and the Mortgage Bankers Association had "by
resolution given their unqualified support" to this suggestion.[47] In addition, the association reprinted an editorial

from the Mankato, Minnesota, *Free Press* which pointed out
the dangers in government domination of banking. This
reprint was distributed to 18,000 newspapers throughout the
country.[48] State bankers associations were also active.
Numerous resolutions were passed and sent to members of
Congress. The Arkansas Bankers Association resolved that
"Title II should be eliminated from the bill and made the
subject of a long, careful, and unbiased study by an impartial agency of recognized integrity and outstanding ability,
to deal with this great phase of our economic life. Such a
committee should be representative of commerce, industry
and banking."[49] Resolutions were also sent by the Oklahoma
Bankers Association, the Indiana Bankers Association, the
Connecticut Bankers Association, and many other state
organizations. Despite all the protests lodged by bankers
and banking association, Senator Glass was reported to
have warned Francis M. Law, president of the First National
Bank of Houston, Texas, that he "had better get some
businessmen here, because we might as well tell you that
the members of Congress feel you bankers are so selfish,
that your testimony is more or less discredited."[50] Bankers
had not reestablished their respected positions in American
life.

   Some members of the banking community came out in
support of Title II of the Banking Act of 1935. *Business Week*
reported that "unexpected support from many Reserve
member bankers for the new banking legislation adds to the
certainty that the measure will pass despite the opposition
of the Carter Glass group to increasing political power over
the country's banking structure." In particular, "unexpected
support among individual bankers for the idea of more in-
dustrialists and fewer bankers on the Reserve Bank boards"
was noted.[51] The secretary of banking for the common-
wealth of Pennsylvania, Luther A. Harr, strongly supported
the measure: "I wish to state most emphatically that I

favor the passage of the Banking Act of 1935 at this session
of Congress. I believe that the prompt passage of this bill,
particularly Title II, is very essential, not only for the
strengthening of our banking system, but to enable our
banking system to function properly and efficiently."[52] On
May 2, Democratic Congressman Thomas F. Ford of California stated to the members of the House of Representatives: "I do not believe the western bankers are opposed to
this bill. In fact some of the leading bankers of the West
that I have talked with are in favor of it."[53] The congressman's belief was borne out by a statement issued by A. P.
Giannini of California's Bank of America. Giannini objected
to the views expressed before the Senate subcommittee by
James P. Warburg: "However typical his attitude may be
taken as that of the New York banker it by no means represents the attitude of many bankers outside New York. . . .
Personally I would rather that this power be exercized by a
public body in the public interest than by the New York
banking fraternity." He continued:

> I am opposed to a government-owned central bank but I support
> the idea of giving the Federal Reserve Board a large degree of
> authority in the system's policies. I think it wise that the Governor
> of the Federal Reserve, the President's representative on the
> Board, his term to run concurrently with that of the President, and
> he as such representative, should sit in on all monetary conferences
> with foreign governments rather than the Governor of the Federal
> Reserve Bank of New York as is the case at present.[54]

In spite of the support of some bankers, the campaign of
protest waged by most bankers accelerated. Commenting on
the role of the bankers in engendering protest against Title II
of the banking bill, Senator Duncan Fletcher, chairman of
the full Senate Banking and Currency Committee, issued a
statement in which he said:

> A number of bankers, editors, pseudoeconomists, and so-called

"financial experts" have bandied the subject back and forth in
the press and through the medium of "form letter" correspondence
for something like two months. Such tactics have resulted in a
wealth of misinformation. Much of this misinformation has been
deliberate and willful.

Fletcher avowed his support of the bill: "In my opinion, the
proposed Banking Act of 1935 is, in all probability, the most
important piece of banking and monetary policy legislation
with which this or any other Congress has dealt." Of the
monetary policy aspect of Title II he said:

> Bankers as a whole are not qualified to determine nor competent
> to administer our monetary policy. They have not been able to
> discern the differences between purely banking functions and
> monetary policy operations. As a whole they have known only
> that money was "easy" or money was "tight" without knowing
> the "whys" and "wherefores" and have been wholly ineffectual
> if not irresponsible in the administration of our monetary policy.[55]

From the time of its introduction, Carter Glass maintained
that the Banking Act of 1935 did not have the president's
support. In March he told Secretary Morgenthau that Roosevelt
had revealed this to him. Morgenthau reported back to the
president and relates in his diary that when the president
was informed of Glass's remark "all the color left the President's face and he said nothing for a few moments." In
reply to the secretary's direct quesion as to the truth of the
statement, Roosevelt categorically denied making a deal with
Glass. According to Morgenthau, "In January he admitted he
had said he wanted only to support the Federal Deposit Insurance bill and unified bank examinations, but on March 4,
he maintained he had added that he was keeping his mind
open about the Federal Reserve." Morgenthau believed that in
spite of Roosevelt's denial, some agreement had in fact been
made.[56] At that time the administration's Relief Bill was
pending before the Glass Appropriations Committee, and it

is not difficult to suspect that Franklin Roosevelt utilized
all the political dexterity and ingenuity at his command to
pacify the senator from Virginia in the interest of this
program.

As the congressional hearings continued, the administration grew impatient with the delay on the banking bill. With
the passage of the Relief Act, the president turned his attention to the problem of banking legislation. It was reported
that Senator Fletcher had quoted him directly as saying
that "he wanted Title II of the proposed banking act passed
in the form it was originally written." *Business Week*
commented:

> At this writing the President has not repudiated Mr. Fletcher's
> statement. It is fair then to assume that the confiscation of our
> banking and credit structure for political purposes is one of the
> legislative schemes which the Administration will undertake to
> force through the present session of Congress.[57]

Shortly thereafter the president clarified his position on
banking legislation. In an April 28 radio address to the nation,
he spoke of the economic problems facing the country. He
called for the enactment of legislation then pending before
Congress, and pointed out that public confidence had been
reestablished in private banking.

> We all know that private banking actually exists by virtue of the
> permission of and regulation by the people as a whole, speaking
> through their government. Wise public policy, however, requires
> not only that banking be safe but that its resources be most fully
> utilized in the economic life of the country. To this end it was
> decided more than 20 years ago that the Government should
> assume the responsibility of providing a means by which the credit
> of the nation might be controlled, not by a few private banking
> institutions but by a body with public prestige and authority. The
> answer to this demand was the Federal Reserve System.

Roosevelt then noted that "twenty years of experience with this system have justified the efforts made to create it."

> But these twenty years have shown by experience definite possibilities for improvement. Certain proposals made to amend the Federal Reserve Act deserve prompt and favorable action by Congress. They are a minimum of wise readjustments of our Federal Reserve System in the light of past experience and present needs.[58]

Despite the president's urging, the Senate hearings dragged on. In mid-May, Secretary Morgenthau gave his testimony. Worried about the outcome of the banking legislation, his thoughts turned to government purchase of Federal Reserve Bank stock. When he had asked the president how he should testify, Roosevelt had told him "to go up to the Hill and say he knew nothing about banking but that he favored unified examination of banks, a permanent plan of deposit insurance, the placing of the Open Market Committee under the Federal Reserve Board in Washington, and government purchase of Federal Reserve stock." Morgenthau did so. After his testimony, reporters asked Roosevelt if he shared the secretary's view on the purchase of the Federal Reserve stock. Off the record, Roosevelt replied, "I think it would solve a great many questions." He recalled that Andrew Jackson's secretary of the Treasury had proposed, during the fight with the Second Bank of the United States, that the government obtain a majority interest in the bank. The president remarked, "That's a hundred years ago but it would have solved the banking situation at that time in a much more satisfactory way."[59] Roosevelt did nothing personally, however, to advance this point of view.

In an effort to speed up the legislation, the president sent a note by special messenger to Senator Fletcher: "Dear Duncan, Can't you keep the Banking Bill in the whole Committee and not refer it to Carter's subcommittee. This would be a great help." And Senator Fletcher replied: "My dear

Mr. President, Yours marked private was duly received and I am giving the matter attention along the lines of your suggestion. The situation is somewhat difficult but I hope we can accomplish results."[60] The bill remained with the subcommittee but pressure was on to expedite the hearings. To counter this pressure, Carter Glass sent a letter to Senator Fletcher:

> We are well aware that it is desirable, if not imperative, that there should be legislation before June 16th on Titles I and III of S.1715: and had your advice and mine been taken these titles would have long since been passed in a separate bill. Title II, as you know, is extremely controversial and is entitled to receive adequate consideration, and the subcommittee is under obligation to hear testimony from those who are seriously affected by its provisions.[61]

With the president actively supporting the banking bill, tension between Carter Glass and the White House increased. In a letter to William Koelsch of the Chase National Bank, Glass wrote, "Your Mr. Aldrich gave splendid testimony before my subcommittee several days ago; but whether the President of the United States will ever read it, much less heed it, may be seriously doubted."[62] The financial press commented on the struggle between the president and the senator. *The Commercial and Financial Chronicle* observed "that current 'polls' of the Senate indicate that the President has control of votes sufficient to pass the bill as it now stands."[63]

While congressional deliberations took place, Marriner Eccles waged a campaign to win the support of the banking community for Title II of the banking bill. On February 12, five days after the bill had been introduced in Congress, he addressed the mid-winter convention of the Ohio Bankers Association. Later that month he met with the executive council of the American Bankers Association. In May he spoke to the New Jersey Bankers Association, and in June to the Pennsylvania Bankers Association. Concerning his campaign to convert the bankers, Eccles later wrote: "I could convince bankers individually of the need for changes in the Reserve System, but when they returned to their own camps, they went native again and accepted the party line."[64]

On June 3, the Senate subcommittee concluded its hearings on the Banking Act of 1935. Action on the banking bill by the full Senate Banking and Currency Committee was delayed further, partly because of Carter Glass' absence from Washington. Interestingly, the senator chose this time to travel outside the capital and to accept a number of honorary degrees. In June Glass spoke to Governor Harrison about the banking bill. He said that the committee's consideration of Title II had been postponed until his return to Washington and that, upon his return, his plan was to amend it "in such a fashion as to make it objectionable to the Administration." He told Harrison, "I think I have them badly whipped both in the subcommittee and in the big committee."[65]

Meanwhile, the July 1 deadline drew near. The administration, the bankers, and the Congress knew that an omnibus banking bill could not be passed in time to afford the relief desired for the banking community as provided in Titles I and III. As early as May 13, Chairman Crowley and Comptroller O'Connor, at a meeting of the Subcommittee on Banking Legislation, supported a proposition made by members of the banking community and advocated by Senator Glass. This proposition called for the immediate passage of Titles I and III, and provided that Title II be held over for a more thorough investigation. Secretary Morgenthau opposed this move. He said they "had been all through that," and that "those titles were just part of the Administration's financial program."[66] To avoid dismemberment of the banking bill, Marriner Eccles sought the aid of the president. Eccles, together with Congressman Goldsborough, prepared a resolution "extending for sixty days the effective date on which the onerous provisions of existing law would go into effect." This extension, he felt, "would relieve the immediate pressure to take Title II out of the bills so that the uncontested titles could pass." Roosevelt agreed to this action and brought pressure on Chairman Steagall of the House Banking and Currency Committee to advance the resolution. Steagall, acting in accordance with the president's wishes, introduced a resolution providing for the necessary time extension. The measure quickly passed in the House of Representatives and the Senate concurred in the action.[67]

On July 2, the Senate version of the Banking Act of 1935 was finally reported out of committee. The measure was presented to the Senate with an amendment in the nature of a substitute, and the committee recommended that, as amended, the bill be passed. Carter Glass had indeed done his utmost to amend Title II of the Banking Act. Every section and almost every paragraph had been changed. The reported bill was greatly altered from that originally introduced and differed substantially from the legislation passed by the House of Representatives. But the revised bill increased the powers of the Federal Reserve Board and gave it a greater degree of supervisory control over the regional Federal Reserve banks. Authority was specifically lodged in Washington. The Senate bill did not streamline the Federal Reserve System in accordance with the provisions originally requested and amended by the House. It endeavored to safeguard the Federal Reserve Board against political domination and to prevent the misuse of Federal Reserve powers by the executive branch of the government. In a press release issued subsequent to the submission of the Senate committee report, Eccles stated:

> As rewritten and reported by the Senate Committee on Banking and Currency, Title II represents a significant and important

recognition of the fundamental principles and purposes of the banking bill as proposed. Therefore, I believe that in its most vital respects it is a distinct advance in the direction of centralized responsibility and authority for the exercise of monetary policy.

He noted the particular improvements provided, and concluded:

> In less fundamental respects I believe that Title II, as reported by the Senate Committee, could and should be improved upon in the interest of practical administration and greater efficiency. As between the bill as enacted by the House and as proposed by the Senate Committee I have every reason to believe that a reasonably satisfactory measure will be worked out.[68]

Although the proposed Senate bill increased the centralization of authority in Washington, it limited the exercise of such authority to a far greater extent than was true in either the original or House bill.

The original bill provided for the annual appointment of Federal Reserve Bank governors by the respective board of each regional bank, and for the appointments to be approved by the Federal Reserve Board. The House version of the bill changed the governor's term to three years, while the Senate version increased it to five years. Both bills retained the provision for board approval of the appointment. The House bill broadened the qualifications for members of the Federal Reserve Board and provided that the governor and vice-governor would be designated by the president, confirmed by the Senate, and would serve until further order of the president. The Senate bill provided for a chairman and vice-chairman, designated by the president and confirmed by the Senate, to serve for a term of four years. The qualifications set forth in existing law for board members were retained in the Senate bill. These qualifications provided specifically for fair representation of financial, agricultural, industrial, and commercial interests and for geographic representation. The bill as introduced and the House version retained the provisions of existing law regarding the size of the board and the length of membership terms. The Senate bill increased the appointed members of the board from six to seven and provided for the removal of the secretary of the Treasury and the comptroller of the Currency as *ex officio* members of the board.

The House bill provided for the creation of an Open Market Advisory Committee composed of five representatives of the Federal Reserve banks. This committee was to consult with and make recommendations to the Federal Reserve Board, which was charged with full responsibility for open market operations. The Senate bill called for an Open Market Committee composed of board members and five representatives of the Federal Reserve banks. The responsibility for open market operations rested with this committee. In addition, the Senate bill compelled full participation by all Federal Reserve banks in open market operations.

The Senate bill concurred with the House bill in granting the board in Washington authority over reserve requirements and in preserving its power to determine and make effective discount rates. Both the House and Senate versions of the bill recognized the need to broaden and liberalize the eligibility requirements with respect to collateral for loans to member banks, and both bills provided adjustments regarding real estate loans by national banks.

A provision in the original bill and in the House bill concerning collateral for Federal Reserve Notes was eliminated from the Senate bill, as was a provision calling for the retirement of Federal Reserve Board members at age 70. Retirement benefits for board members were also eliminated from the Senate bill. The mandate given by the House bill to the Federal Reserve Board to exercise its powers in such manner as to promote conditions conducive to business stability was completely deleted from the Senate version.

The bill as reported by the Senate Banking and Currency Committee was somewhat better than the administraton had expected. It did not give the Federal Reserve Board the clear mandate for promoting economic stability that Governor Eccles desired, and in many particulars was much weaker than the bill enacted by the House. With respect to practical administration and greater efficiency of operations, modifications were considered a necessity. From July 23 to July 26, the amended bill was debated by the Senate. Additional amendments were proposed from the Senate floor but none were approved. During the Senate debate, the administration made no move to have the amended bill repudiated or revised. Its strategy was to wait for Senate passage and then to fight for an improved bill in the conference committee. On July 26, the Senate debate was concluded and the much amended Banking Act of 1935 was approved. The bill was sent to the House of Representatives where the Senate amendments were rejected. Conferees were appointed by both houses of Congress to meet and resolve the differences between the two bills.[69]

In his autobiography, Marriner Eccles elucidated the strategy employed to solidify the advance made toward centralization of Federal Reserve control in Washington and to combat the undesirable features of the Senate version of the bill. Although representatives from the Office of the Comptroller of the Currency and the Federal Deposit Insurance Corporation participated in the conference proceedings, no representatives of the Federal Reserve System were allowed to attend. As a result, Congressman Goldsborough, one of the House conferees, assumed personal responsibility for the fate of Title II. Eccles relates:

> Before Goldsborough went into the conference committee I listed all the provisions in the House bill and also weighed the relative

importance of each provision. In a parallel column I listed the
points in the Senate bill and again weighed them in order of their
relative importance. I then advised Goldsborough to cling to the
first five basic provisions of the House bill even if he had to
capitulate on all other points. Goldsborough met with me after
each conference to discuss the strategy of give and take for the
next day. I doubt whether any other member of the conference
committee had weighed the relative importance of each provision.
Glass certainly did not do so. Each provision in the bill was a self
contained good for him, isolated in its effect from any other
provision.[70]

The bill that emerged from the conference committee retained the Senate bill's amendment advancing centralization
of Federal Reserve authority in Washington. Adjustments
were made to facilitate the administration and efficiency of
Federal Reserve operations. The bill did not reinstate the
broad power which the House bill gave to the Federal Reserve
Board. On the positive side, the compromise bill did con-
firm completely the public nature of the Federal Reserve
System and established the fact that Carter Glass, as well as
the administration, favored a Federal Reserve System free
from the banking community's domination. However, the
senator from Virginia also favored a Federal Reserve System
free from the domination of the New Deal administration.

Although the provisions of Title I and Title III of the
House and Senate versions of the Banking Act did not differ
substantially from one another, two particular provisions
were controversial. A Senate amendment to Title III had
removed the restrictions placed on commercial banks with
respect to underwriting securities. Roosevelt held strong
views on this subject. Early in July, he sent a letter to
Carter Glass concerning the amendment: "I should like very
much to talk to you about banks underwriting securities.
You have had a long period of intimate contact with banking
legislation, but I have seen more rotten practices among banks

in New York City than you have. Regulations and penalties will not stop them if they want to resume speculation."[71] Despite this opposition, the provision remained in the bill. On August 8, the president again wrote to Senator Glass:

> As to underwriting of securities by banks, I am frankly wholly opposed. The provision in the Senate bill for a so-called safeguard through open market sales is not a safeguard. If you were not of such a trusting and unsuspicious nature, and if you had my experience with certain elements in certain places you would know that the old abuses would come back if underwriting were restored in any shape, manner or form.
>
> One other thought—two years ago you and I were agreed that the underwriting of securities never was and never should be a legitimate right or action on the part of commercial banks. I honestly think a great question of principle is involved and I cannot change my opinion, especially as it is based on a great many years of practical experience in connection with these banking institutions which conducted such underwriting in the past.[72]

Although the provision remained in the bill as passed by the Senate, the president's wishes ultimately prevailed, and, as a direct result of his intercession, the securities underwriting provision was stricken from the conference committee's compromise bill.

A second controversial provision was contained in Title I of the Senate bill. This provision pertained to compulsory membership in the Federal Reserve System for all banks joining the Federal Deposit Insurance Corporation. This requirement had been eliminated in the House bill but was reinstated in the Senate bill and survived the conference committee's deliberations. Yet, the committee did amend the provision so that the time allowed for banks to join the Federal Reserve System was extended from 1937 to 1942, and was made applicable to state banks with deposits of $1 million or more. When the conference report came up for debate in the House, Chairman Steagall, who had fought against the provision, told the House members that "when this plan is deferred until 1942 those who have opposed it are not seriously disturbed. The engagement has been entered into under duress, and the marriage ceremony will not take place, nor will the union be completed until 1942. This would be a long time to consummate a marriage contract. . . . We have notice of the plan and can take every action deemed wise. Of course it will never go into effect then or later."[73] The chairman was quite right. In the years that followed, the time stipulation was repeatedly extended and in 1939 the provision was eliminated from the law.

The compromise bill was reported out of the conference committee on August 17. After a brief debate in the House of Representatives and with no debate whatsoever in the Senate, the bill was passed by both houses.[74] On August 23, the president signed the Banking Act of 1935 into law. As enacted, Title II of the measure provided for basic changes in the Federal Reserve System. Under the new law, the Federal Reserve Board was replaced by the board of governors of the Federal Reserve System composed of seven members, appointed by the president, and confirmed by the Senate. The original appointments were to be scheduled for terms of from two to fourteen years so that not more than one would expire in any two-year period. At the insistence of Carter Glass, the *ex officio* membership of the secretary of the Treasury and the comptroller of the Currency was terminated. The chief executive officer would henceforth be a chairman designated by the president to serve for a term of four years.

The new law gave recognition to existing conditions with respect to the executive authority of the Federal Reserve banks. The title of governor was changed to president; this executive would be appointed by the boards of directors of the individual Federal Reserve banks for a five-year term, subject to the approval of the board of governors in Washington. The existing Federal Open Market Committee, composed of twelve governors of the Federal Reserve banks, was abolished and replaced by a new Federal Open Market Committee consisting of the board of governors and five representatives of the Federal Reserve banks, to be selected annually through the combined efforts of the boards of directors of the regional banks. This Federal Open Market Committee was empowered to formulate open market policy and no Federal Reserve Bank was permitted to engage, or to decline to engage, in open market operations except in accordance with the recommendation of the Federal Open Market Committee. In addition, the board of governors was granted increased powers over Reserve requirements and the Federal Reserve banks were granted authority, under regulation of the board of governors, to make advances on any "satisfactory" as well as eligible paper to member banks. Moreover, restrictions on real estate loans by national banks were liberalized. With respect to membership in the Federal Reserve System, the board of governors was authorized to waive requirements relating to the admission of state banks that had deposits of $1 million or more and that were required to become members of the system prior to July 1, 1942, in accordance with the amendment to Title I of the act dealing with the Federal Deposit Insurance Corporation.

Titles I and III of the new law brought the desired relief to the banking community. The FDIC assessments were adjusted and the way was cleared for the corporation to begin operations. Title III extended the deadline date for executive officers of member banks to divest themselves of loans from their own institutions, and eased other restrictions enacted by the Banking Act of 1933. Other necessary technical amendments required to clarify and improve existing law were covered by this title.

Upon its enactment, the Banking Act of 1935 received

praise from the bankers, the administration, and the Congress. Rudolph Hecht, on behalf of the American Bankers Association, commented that "on the whole the Banking Act of 1935 is an acceptable piece of legislation," and that the new law was "basically sound and merits confidence on the part of the banks."[75] Marriner Eccles, chief proponent for the administration's banking bill, remarked: "Considering the objectives and purposes of the legislation as originally proposed and finally enacted, I am very well satisfied with the outcome."[76] When the bill was signed into law, Carter Glass made no statement, but at a later date he wrote to a friend: "I have said and still maintain that we did not leave enough of the Eccles bill with which to light a cigarette. Of course a better bill than that enacted could have been written; but writing a bill and getting it through both houses of Congress are two entirely different propositions."[77]

The Banking Act of 1935, although altered from the original draft, advanced the centralization of power and control over banking. It lodged responsibility specifically in Washington and brought the world of banking more firmly in line with the government program of monetary management and credit control. As a result, almost as a byproduct, federal control over banking was greatly augmented.

The essence of the debate on Title II was closely related to questions of monetary management and credit control. With a more powerful Federal Reserve Board and a new federal banking agency in the Federal Deposit Insurance Corporation, far more banks were brought closer to the reality of federal supervision. In their opposition to the Banking Act of 1935, bankers had united as never before against the federal government's incursions into banking. Aided by Carter Glass's determination to prevent a New Deal takeover of the Federal Reserve System, the bankers had achieved a degree of success. On the whole, however, the administration was by far the greater victor.

NOTES

1. *Congressional Record*, LXXIX, p. 1501.
2. Ibid., p. 1513.
3. "Morgenthau Diaries," November 26, 1934.
4. Ibid., December 10, 1934.
5. Ibid., December 28, 1934.
6. Ibid., November 2, 1934.
7. Marriner S. Eccles (S Hyman, ed.), *Beckoning Frontiers, Public and Personal Recollections* New York, 1951), p. 175. Copyright 1951 by Alfred A. Knopf, Inc. All quotations from this work are quoted by permission of the publisher.
8. Ibid., pp. 191-193.
9. "Morgenthau Diaries," December 19, 1934.
10. Ibid., January 17, 1935.
11. Ibid., January 30, 1935.
12. Eccles, *Beckoning Frontiers*, p. 197.
13. "Morgenthau Diaries," February 4, 1935.
14. *The Journal of Commerce*, February 6, 1935.
15. *The Wall Street Journal*, February 6, 1935.
16. *Business Week*, February 9, 1935, p. 10.
17. U.S. House of Representatives, Banking and Currency Committee, 74th Congress, 1st Session, *Banking Act of 1935, Hearings . . . on H.R. 5357* (Washington, D.C., 1935), pp. 513-516.
18. *Congressional Record*, LXXIX, p. 6096.
19. Eccles, *Beckoning Frontiers*, p. 228.
20. *Congressional Record*, LXXIX, p. 7270.
21. *Commercial and Financial Chronicle*, CXL (February 16, 1935), p. 1013.
22. *Business Week*, February 23, 1935, p. 32.
23. Ibid., March 30, 1935, p. 32.
24. *The Texas Bankers Record*, XXV (April 1935), p. II.
25. *The Commercial and Financial Chronicle*, CXL (March 30, 1935), p. 2062.
26. Federal Reserve Bank of New York, Board of Directors, Memorandum of Meeting, February 7, 1935, "Discussion Notes," Harrison Papers.
27. Federal Reserve Bank of New York, Executive Committee, Memorandum of Meeting, February 11, 1935, ibid.
28. *The New York Times*, February 13, 1935.
29. Glass to M. B. Wellborn, February 16, 1935, Box 304, Glass Papers.

30. Glass to Ralph Robey, March 13, 1935, ibid.

31. Glass to Willis, April 3, 1935, Box 382, ibid.

32. Eccles, *Beckoning Frontiers,* p. 204.

33. *Congressional Record,* LXXIX, p. 6213.

34. Harrison to Glass, March 22, 1935, Personal Correspondence, Glass Folder, Harrison Papers.

35. Harrison to Glass, February 19, 1935, ibid.

36. U.S. Senate, Banking and Currency Subcommittee, 74th Congress, 1st Session, *Banking Act of 1935, Hearings . . . on S. 1715 and H.R. 7617* (Washington, D.C., 1935), p. 71.

37. Ibid., p. 193.

38. Ibid., pp. 386-422.

39. Ibid., pp. 544-549.

40. The Girard Trust Company, *The Girard Letter,* April 1935, Box 304, Glass Papers.

41. *The Bankers Magazine,* CXXX (May 1935), p. 517.

42. Guaranty Trust Company of New York, *The Banking Bill of 1935 in Its Relation to Sound Business and Banking* (n.p., n.d.), pp. 3-9.

43. Bankers Trust Company, *The Proposed Banking Act of 1935* (n.p., 1935), p. 8.

44. Robert D. Brewer, President, The Merchants National Bank of Boston to Depositors and Stockholders, June 6, 1935, Box 344, Glass Papers.

45. *The Literary Digest,* CXIX (May 25, 1935), p. 40.

46. U.S. Senate, Banking and Currency Subcommittee, 74th Congress, 1st Session, *Banking Act of 1935, Hearings . . . on S.1715 and H.R. 7617* (Washington, D.C., 1935), p. 516.

47. The Association of Reserve City Bankers, *Proceedings of 24th Annual Convention* (n.p. 1935), p. 41.

48. Ibid., *Proceedings of 25th Annual Convention* (n.p., 1936), p. 6.

49. Arkansas Bankers Association, "Resolution," May 10, 1935, U.S. Senate Records, Record Group 46, U.S. National Archives and Records Service,

50. Francis M. Law, "The Future of Banking," *The Texas Bankers Record,* XXV (June 1935), p. 22.

51. *Business Week,* March 2, 1935, p. 7.

52. Harr to Senator Duncan Fletcher, June 6, 1935, U.S. Senate Records, Record Group 46, U.S. National Archives and Records Service.

53. *Congressional Record,* LXXIX, p. 6802.

54. *The Commercial and Financial Chronicle,* CXL (May 4, 1935), p. 2967.

55. *Congressional Record,* LXXIX, pp. 6102-6104.

56. "Morgenthau Diaries," March 18, 1933.

57. *Business Week,* April 27, 1935, p. 36.

58. *Congressional Record,* LXXIX, p. 6512.

59. "Morgenthau Diaries," May 15, 1935; Arthur M. Schlesinger, Jr., *The Age of Roosevelt,* 3 vols. (Boston, Mass., 1957-1960), II, pp. 290-300.

60. Roosevelt to Fletcher, May 14, 1935; Fletcher to Roosevelt, May 14,

1935, President's Personal File, Folder 1358, Roosevelt Papers.

61. Glass to Fletcher, May 15, 1935, Box 304, Glass Papers.

62. Glass to Koelsch, May 20, 1935, Box 334, ibid.

63. *The Commercial and Financial Chronicle,* CXL (May 25, 1935), p. 3434.

64. Eccles, *Beckoning Frontiers,* p. 202.

65. Harrison to Personal Files, June 16, 1935, "Conversations," Harrison Papers.

66. "Morgenthau Diaries," May 13, 1935.

67. Eccles, *Beckoning Frontiers,* 218-219; *Congressional Record,* LXXIX, p. 11935.

68. *The New York Times,* July 4, 1935.

69. *Congressional Record,* LXXIX, pp. 11935, 12005.

70. Eccles, *Beckoning Frontiers,* pp. 220-221.

71. *F.D.R. Personal Letters,* III, p. 491.

72. Roosevelt to Glass, August 8, 1935, Box 8, Glass Papers.

73. *Congressional Record,* LXXIX, p. 13705.

74. Ibid., pp. 13655, 13711.

75. *The Journal of Commerce,* August 24, 1935.

76. *The Wall Street Journal,* August 24, 1935.

77. Glass to Frederick E. Lee, December 1, 1935, Box 304, Glass Papers.

Conclusions

From 1930 to 1935, bank reform legislation was of immediate concern to the banking community. When Franklin Roosevelt took office on March 4, 1933, banking conditions had sunk to their lowest level in the nation's history. For three years prior to his inauguration, studies and investigations had taken place and legislative reforms had been proposed. Bankers had appeared before congressional committees to argue for and against specific provisions in the remedial legislation, but as a group with divided interests and irreconcilable differences they found it impossible to unite upon a banker-sponsored program of reform. The variety of banking institutions and the dual banking system argued against a united effort.

Yet, beneath the surface of the banking picture there were stirrings of discontent. Individual bankers voiced their dissatisfaction with the status quo. They denounced bad banking, lax supervision, unfair competition, and malpractices. Some bankers expressed their desire to see all commercial banks unified into one federal system. Tradition, however, stood in the path of increased federal supervision of banking. History did not support the premise that a government in Washington was the logical agent to create the most efficient and soundest banking system possible. From the time of the demise of the Second Bank of the United

States in 1836, the federal government had taken only two steps in the field of banking. At the outbreak of the Civil War, the National Bank Act was passed, primarily to aid in financing the war; this law also gave the country a uniform and reasonably stable currency. Fifty years later, in 1913, the Federal Reserve System was established to prevent panics and provide an elastic currency. From 1913 to 1933, no additional major banking laws were enacted, and no other advancements were made pertaining to federal supervision of banking. In the twenty-year period that followed the enactment of the Federal Reserve Act, conditions in the American nation had changed radically. A world war had been fought and won, a period of growth had followed, a decade of speculative frenzy culminating in a stock market crash had been experienced, and a depression of unprecedented proportions had taken hold. Still the banking laws remained unchanged. Traditional bankers supported long-accepted banking views. Their strength was augmented by the American tradition of the dual banking system. State banks, established under state laws, for the most part small-unit banks serving local communities, offered the greatest opposition to further extension of the federal government into banking. State governments supported this position, and in the halls of Congress the doctrine of states' rights was a powerful weapon against those who sought to impair the dual banking system.

With the stock market crash, the depression, and the banking crisis, bankers lost the initiative to bring about reforms of their choosing. The people, angered and dismayed by the banking crisis, speaking through their representatives in Washington, demanded reform and reform was forthcoming. The Emergency Banking Act and the Banking Act of 1933 were the result of this demand. In the early days of the Roosevelt administration, the banking community was not ignored. At the time of the banking crisis, an immediate

call went out to leading bankers to assemble in Washington
to help seek a solution to the bank debacle. The administration found that with few exceptions bankers had no solution
to the banking problems. As a result, a coalition of the old
and new administrations, aided by George Harrison of the
Federal Reserve Bank of New York, drafted the Emergency
Banking Act. The Roosevelt forces moved quickly, firmly,
and with courageous optimism to reassure the people. When
the banks reopened, a surge of confidence swept the country and carried in its wake the passage of the Banking Act
of 1933. In conjunction with the Banking Act of 1933, no
hearings were held, and no opportunity was given the bankers
to voice their views or defend themselves against the general
public indignation which had resulted from the actions of a
small minority among them. Individual bankers and bankers
associations did speak out vigorously on the controversial
provisions of the legislation. Almost with a single voice they
opposed the deposit insurance feature of the bill, but neither
the bankers nor the administration, acting independently or
collectively, could defeat a measure that had gained such
strong public support.

Badly shaken by the stock market crash, the depth of the
depression, and the resulting stresses on the banking business,
the banking community turned extremely conservative. While
in the 1920s loans had been granted much too liberally, the
pendulum in the 1930s swung to an overly stringent policy.
The administration, determined on credit expansion, an end
to deflation, and economic rehabilitation, exhorted the
bankers to participate fully in the New Deal recovery programs. The response of the banking industry was constrained
by the events of the recent past and apprehensions for the
future. To many bankers the Roosevelt programs of deficit
spending, public relief, social rehabilitation, and monetary
management were radical in the extreme. The bankers supported a balanced budget, personal initiative, private indus-

try, and the gold dollar. Without these, many bankers firmly believed the country was headed for bankruptcy. Moreover, most bankers detested the New Deal advisers who flocked to Washington, and they bitterly resented the president's unkind words about the banking industry. Franklin Roosevelt had not banished fear from the banking community but had, in fact, greatly augmented the apprehensions of the banking world. His economic policies, social reforms, and bureaucratic government aroused consternation and alarm in banking circles. The possibility of complete government control of banking was never far from the bankers' thoughts. Small bankers, serving local communities, feared the federal government could in no way understand the local needs of such communities. Bankers from large institutions, proud of their influence and their prerogatives under existing law, did not want to relinquish their power to what many considered to be a radical government in Washington.

The banking community failed to comprehend the president's own philosophy of banking. There is little evidence to suggest that Roosevelt ever seriously considered nationalization of the banking system, although he was quick to use the possibility as a threat to bring bankers in line with the New Deal programs, and he did not hesitate to advocate firmly what he believed to be necessary changes in the banking laws. There is much to support the premise that, in his attitude and actions on bank reform, Roosevelt revealed his most conservative inclinations. The opinions he expressed, both in public and private, indicate this to be the case. He was, of course, incensed at bad banking, mismanagement, and malpractices. So too were the bankers. He supported the dual banking system. So too did most bankers. Throughout the period of crisis, he went out of his way to see that state banks received help on the same basis as that rendered to national banks and members of the Federal Reserve System, thus giving lie to the rumor that a government-owned and

-operated bank had his support. In many ways, Carter Glass, the Jeffersonian Democrat who opposed the Banking Act of 1935, was a stronger advocate of federal control over banking than was Franklin Roosevelt. Glass favored the extension of branch banking by national banks; the president did not. Glass worked actively for the unification of commercial banking under the Federal Reserve System; again the president did not. Glass fought against aid to state banks; the president insisted it should be granted. Glass thought the dual banking system an abomination; the president gave it his support. In the years that followed the enactment of the Banking Act of 1935, plans for unification of the banking system were often urged upon the president. Roosevelt took no action to advance such proposals, and showed no inclination to support additional major reforms of the federal banking laws. In discussing the president's inertia in this area, Marriner Eccles suggests that the dual banking system "was held in nostalgic affection by Roosevelt." He writes:

> In his view the state nonmember banks represented the small democratically controlled institutions, responsive to local needs, with officers who had the welfare of the homefolks at heart. For some curious reason the Federal Reserve, on the other hand, represented for him the banking giants, and in a way, he saw the Banking Act of 1935 as a means of curbing the giants. To unify the whole banking system, however, implied two things in Roosevelt's mind. First it implied the end of the state banking system. And second, by forcing the small banks into the Reserve System, it implied a condition favorable to their destruction by the giants.[1]

Roosevelt never forcefully set forth his own views on banking. He made few speeches on the subject, and there is every indication that, in and of itself, banking held little attraction for him. Even so, he was prepared to utilize the banking industry to further the goals of the New Deal programs—those very programs which were so abhorrent to so many bankers. To the president and his advisers, economic recovery was the first priority. An unbalanced budget, public relief, and departure from gold were used to fight the depression and restore economic stability. To bankers, deficit financing, public spending, and devaluation were quickly identified with New Deal radicalism. The record shows that Roosevelt did not delve deeply into economic theory. He was a pragmatic politician and a strong executive who did not fear experimentation. Faced with a unique economic disaster, it was inevitable that his actions and his policies would cause dismay and raise alarm, and that a majority of bankers would stand in strong opposition to the New Deal administration.

Whereas the bankers did not understand the president, the president understood the bankers all too well. He knew that there were many features in the New Deal program that they would actively oppose. In his public addresses, he chided them and belittled them, and seemed to take great delight in doing so. Yet, the White House door was frequently open to members of the banking fraternity, and the president maintained friendly correspondence with many bankers. Roosevelt was born and bred to the world of bankers and businessmen. If he did not always agree with their views, he did not underestimate the value of their opinions. Through his contact with such men as George Harrison of the Federal Reserve Bank of New York, Winthrop Aldrich of the Chase National Bank, and James Perkins of the National City Bank, the president kept his finger on the pulse of the banking world. The knowledge gained was useful in resolving problems and formulating action with respect to banking as well as other economic matters.

In 1913, Woodrow Wilson, in his first inaugural address, spoke of reform. He said:

> We shall restore, not destroy. We shall deal with our economic

system as it is, and as it may be modified, not as it might be if we had a clean sheet of paper to write upon, and step by step, we shall make it what it should be, in the spirit of those who question and seek counsel and knowledge, not shallow self satisfaction nor the excitement of excursions wither they cannot tell.[2]

Woodrow Wilson upheld this principle in supporting the establishment of the Federal Reserve System. Roosevelt followed in the same tradition with regard to the bank reforms advocated during the New Deal administration. A coordinated and cooperating banking industry was an urgent necessity in the battle against the continuing depression. Under Roosevelt's leadership, it was the choice of the federal government to modify and rectify the existing banking system rather than build anew as many advocated. In the period of crisis, the existing structure was resuscitated and sustained by the enactment of the Emergency Banking Act. Under the Banking Act of 1933, bank supervision was strengthened and revitalized. With the enactment of the Banking Act of 1935, bank control was firmly centralized in Washington. Nevertheless, throughout relief, recovery, and reform, the structure of the American banking system held firm.

The laws enacted under the Roosevelt administration brought the banking system of the country face to face with the realities of the new era. Under the Banking Act of 1935, the Federal Reserve System was to play an increasing role in stabilizing the economic heartbeat of the nation. Shortly after he had signed this law, the president said:

A rudimentary concept of credit control appropriate for financing the economic life of a nation of 3,000,000 people can hardly be urged as a means of directing and protecting the welfare of our twentieth century industrialism. The simple banking rules of Hamilton's day . . . fail to protect the millions of individual depositors of a great modern banking institution. And so it goes

> through all the range of economic life. Aggressive enterprise and
> shrewd invention have been at work on our economic machine.
> Our rules of conduct for the operation of that machine must be
> subjected to the same constant development.[3]

The changes in the Federal Reserve, effected within the established framework, took place on February 1, 1936. The
old board retired and the new board of governors took over.
Marriner Eccles was reappointed and guided the system through
the remainder of the depression and into the period of World
War II.

In the fight against the Banking Act of 1935, the bankers
centered their opposition on changes in the Federal Reserve
System. They achieved a measure of success. Far better
united than in the past, and with the strong support of
Carter Glass, they forced the administration to retreat on
many points. Yet, as in the past, and despite warnings from
members of their own fraternity, their weakness lay in their
failure to develop a program of their own to replace that
which they denounced. Of the battle that they won, Walter
Lippmann observed that it constituted a victory for Eccles
"dressed up as a defeat."[4]

Under the Roosevelt administration, the Federal Deposit
Insurance Corporation was solidly established as part of the
American banking scene, and control of the Federal Reserve
System was firmly centralized in Washington. Bank supervision was increased and more banking practices were brought
within the scope of the national government. In the years to
come, the bankers, cast in the role of the loyal opposition,
used the strength of their opinions not only to temper the
national administration but also to moderate the remedies and
reforms advocated by liberal and radical elements, both in
and out of Congress. Throughout the 1930s proposals
advocating government ownership of the banks continued.
Those introduced in Congress seldom emerged from committee, and others did not even achieve legislative status. Yet, it

is possible that had Roosevelt or the bankers been less firm in their acceptance of the established system, enactment of far more radical banking legislation might well have been achieved during the Roosevelt administration.

NOTES

1. Eccles, *Beckoning Frontiers*, p. 269.

2. *Congressional Record*, L, p. 3.

3. Rosenman, *The Public Papers and Addresses of Franklin D. Roosevelt*, IV, p. 336.

4. William E. Leuchtenberg, *Franklin D. Roosevelt and the New Deal, 1932-1940* (New York, 1963), p. 160.

Bibliography

This bibliography is not intended as a comprehensive coverage of the literature pertaining to the history of the Great Depression, the Roosevelt era, or money and banking. A great number of primary sources and secondary works were consulted in researching this topic. Those that proved to be most useful have been cited in the notes; the bibliographic entries have been restricted to these works.

UNPUBLISHED MANUSCRIPT SOURCES

Glass, Carter [Member of Senate Banking and Currency Committee].
   Glass Papers. Alderman Library, University of Virginia,
   Charlottesville, Va.
Hamlin, Charles S. [Member of Federal Reserve Board]. The Family
   Papers of Charles S. Hamlin. Library of Congress, Washington, D.C.
Harrison, George L. [Governor of Federal Reserve Bank of New York].
   Harrison Papers, Butler Library, Columbia University, New York, N.Y.
Mills, Ogden L. [Secretary of the Treasury, Hoover Administration].
   Mills Papers. Library of Congress, Washington, D.C.
Morgenthau, Henry, Jr. [Secretary of the Treasury, Roosevelt Admin-
   istration]. "Diary," 1933-1935. Franklin D. Roosevelt Library,
   Hyde Park, N.Y.
Roosevelt, Franklin D. [President of the United States]. Roosevelt
   Papers. Franklin D. Roosevelt Library, Hyde Park, N.Y.
United States Department of Commerce, Records of the Secretary,

Record Group 40. United States National Archives and Records
Service, Washington, D.C.

United States Senate, Records, Record Group 46. United States
National Archives and Records Service, Washington, D.C.

GOVERNMENT DOCUMENTS

Federal Reserve Board. *Annual Report*. Washington, D.C., 1929-1935.

————. *Banking and Monetary Statistics*. Washington, D.C., 1943.

————. *Federal Reserve Bulletin*. Washington, D.C., 1929-1935.

Lewis, E. A., compiler. *Federal Reserve Act of 1913 with Amendments
and Laws Relating to Banking*. Washington, D.C., 1952.

United States Commerce Department. *Historical Statistics of the
United States: Colonial Times to 1957*. Washington, D.C., 1960.

United States Comptroller of the Currency. *Annual Report*.
Washington, D.C., 1929-1935.

United States Congress. *Congressional Record*. 116 vols. Washington,
D.C., 1873–

United States House of Representatives, Banking and Currency Committee, 71st Congress, 2d Session. *Branch, Chain and Group Banking, Hearings . . . under H. Res. 141*. 2 vols. Washington, D.C., 1930.

————, 74th Congress, 1st Session. *Banking Act of 1935, Hearings
on H.R. 5357 . . .* Washington, D.C., 1935.

United States House of Representatives, Banking and Currency Sub-
committee, 72nd Congress, 1st Session. *To Provide a Guaranty
Fund for Depositors in Banks, Hearings . . . H.R. (10241) 11362*.
Washington, D.C., 1932.

United States Senate, Banking and Currency Subcommittee, 71st
Congress, 3rd Session. *Operations of the National and Federal
Reserve Banking Systems, Hearings pursuant to Senate Res. 71 . . .*
7 parts. Washington, D.C., 1931.

————, 74th Congress, 1st Session. *Banking Act of 1935, Hearings . . .
on S.1715 and H.R.7617 . . .* Washington, D.C., 1935.

United States Treasury Department. *Annual Report*. Washington,
D.C., 1929-1935.

[United States Treasury Department.] *Documents and Statements
Pertaining to the Banking Emergency . . .* 2 parts. Washington,
D.C., 1933.

MEMOIRS, DIARIES AND CONTEMPORARY ACCOUNTS

Unpublished

Bruere, Henry [President of the Bowry Savings Bank]. "Reminiscences." Oral History Collection, Columbia University, New York, 1949.

Meyer, Eugene [Governor of the Federal Reserve Board]. "Reminisces." Oral History Collection, Columbia University, New York, n.d.

Reynolds, Jackson E. [President of the First National Bank of New York]. "Reminiscences." Oral History Collection, Columbia University, New York, 1949.

Tugwell, Rexford G. [Member of the Roosevelt Brain Trust]. "Reminiscences." Oral History Collection, Columbia University, New York, 1950.

Published

Berle, A. A., Jr. *The Future of American Banking.* Lake George, N.Y., 1933.

Blum, J. M. *From the Morgenthau Diaries, Years of Crisis, 1928-1938.* New York, 1959.

Eccles, M. S. (Hyman, S., editor) *Beckoning Frontiers, Public and Personal Recollections.* New York, 1951.

Hoover, Herbert. *The Memoirs of Herbert Hoover.* 3 vols. New York, 1951-1952.

Lippmann, Walter. *Interpretations 1933-1935.* New York, 1936.

Meyer, W. S., editor. *The State Papers and Other Public Writings of Herbert Hoover.* 2 vols. Garden City, N.Y., 1934.

Mills, Ogden. *Credit and Confidence, An Address . . . at the Annual Meeting of the American Acceptance Council.* New York, 1932.

Moley, Raymond. *After Seven Years.* New York, 1939.

O'Connor, J.F.T. *The Banking Crisis and Recovery Under the Roosevelt Administration.* Chicago, Ill., 1938.

Roosevelt, Elliott, editor. *F.D.R.: His Personal Letters, 1905-1945.* 4 vols. New York, 1947-1950.

Roosevelt, Franklin D. *Looking Forward.* New York [1933].

————. *On Our Way.* New York [1934].

Rosenman, S. I., editor. *The Public Papers and Addresses of Franklin D. Roosevelt.* 13 vols. New York, 1938-1950.

TRADE LITERATURE AND BANKERS ASSOCIATION REPORTS

Agnew, A. C. "Some Thoughts About the Future of American Banking," *The California Banker,* XIV (June 1933), pp. 193-197.

Aldrich, W. W. *Suggestions for Improving the Banking System.* n.p., 1933.

American Banker. New York, 1932-1935.

American Bankers Association. *Reports of Annual Convention.* 1929-1936.

Bankers Trust Company. *The Proposed Banking Act of 1935.* n.p., 1935.

Bradford, F. A. "Futility of Deposit Guaranty Laws," *The Bankers Magazine,* CXXVI (June 1933), pp. 537-539.

California Bankers Association. *The California Banker.* 1932-1935.

Doan, R. E. "A Challenge to Bankers," *The Bankers Magazine,* CXXVII (April 1934), pp. 369-374.

Guaranty Trust Company of New York. *The Banking Bill of 1935 in Its Relation to Sound Banking and Business.* n.p., n.d.

Heflebower, R. A. "Should Banks Take the Blame," *The Bankers Magazine,* CXXVII (July 1933), pp. 18-22.

Investment Bankers Association of America. *Proceedings of the Annual Convention.* 1930-1935.

Law, F. M. "The Future of Banking," *The Texas Bankers Record,* XXV (June 1933), p. 2123.

Maryland Bankers Association. *Proceedings of the Annual Convention.* 1932-1935.

McLaughlin, G. V. "A Legislative Program for Banking, The Need for Revision of the Glass Steagall Act," *The Bankers Magazine,* CXXVII (November 1933), pp. 495-500.

Missouri Bankers Association. *Proceedings of the Annual Convention.* 1932-1935.

New York State Bankers Association. *Proceedings of the Annual Convention.* 1932-1935.

Sissons, F. H. "How We May Have Safer Banks, The Solution Does Not Lie in the Government Guaranty of Deposits," *The Bankers Magazine,* CXXVI (June 1933), pp. 563-564.

Texas Bankers Association. "Proceedings of 50th Annual Convention," *The Texas Bankers Record,* XXVI (June 1934), pp. 5-60.

———. *The Texas Bankers Record.* 1932-1935.

The Bankers Magazine, Boston, Mass., 1930-1935.

The Commercial and Financial Chronicle. New York, 1932-1935.

The Magazine of Wall Street. New York, 1929-1935.

The Southern Banker. Atlanta, Ga., 1932-1934.

Virginia Bankers Association. *Proceedings of the Annual Convention.* 1933-1935.

SECONDARY WORKS

American Bankers Association. *The Commercial Banking Community.* Englewood Cliffs, N.J., 1962.

Bogen, J. I., and Nadler, Marcus. *The Banking Crisis: The End of an Epoch.* New York, 1933.

Bradford, F. A. *Money and Banking.* New York, 1941.

Burns, J. M. *Roosevelt, The Lion and the Fox.* New York, 1956.

Chapman, C. C. *The Development of American Business and Banking Thought 1913-1936.* Revised edition. London, 1936.

Colt, C. C., and Keith, N. S. *28 Days, A History of the Banking Crisis.* New York, 1933.

Fischer, Gerald. *American Banking Structure.* New York, 1966.

Fusfeld, D. R. *Economic Thought of Franklin D. Roosevelt and the Origin of the New Deal.* New York, 1956.

Greer, T. H. *What Roosevelt Thought.* Lansing, Mich., 1958.

James, Marquis, and James, B. R. *Biography of a Bank, The Story of Bank of America N.T. & S.A.* New York, 1954.

Leuchtenberg, W. E. *Franklin D. Roosevelt and the New Deal, 1932-1940.* New York, 1963.

Lindley, E. K. *Halfway With Roosevelt.* New York, 1936.

————. *The Roosevelt Revolution, First Phase.* New York, 1933.

Mitchell, Broadus. *Depression Decade.* New York, 1947.

Paris, J. D. *Monetary Policies of the United States 1932-1938.* New York, 1938.

Piquet, H. *Outline of the New Deal Legislation of 1933-1934.* New York, 1934.

Prochnow, H. V., editor. *The Federal Reserve System.* New York, 1960.

Reeve, J. E. *Monetary Reform Movements, A Survey of Recent Plans and Panaceas.* Washington, D.C. [1943].

Schlesinger, A. M., Jr. *The Age of Roosevelt.* 3 vols. Boston, Mass. 1957-1960.

Schneider, W. M. *The American Bankers Association, Its Past and Present.* Washington, D.C. [1956].

Schroeder, J. J. *They Made Banking History, The Association of Reserve City Bankers 1911-1960.* Chicago, Ill. [1962].

Smith, Rixley, and Beasley, Norman. *Carter Glass, A Biography.* New York, 1939.

Taus, Esther. *Central Banking Functions of the United States Treasury. 1789-1941.* New York, 1943.

Tugwell, R. G. *The Democratic Roosevelt, A Biography of Franklin D. Roosevelt.* New York, 1943.

Willis, H. P., editor. *The Banking Situation.* New York, 1934.

GENERAL PERIODICALS

Ballantine, A. A. "When All the Banks Closed," *Harvard Business Review,* XXVI (March 1948), pp. 129-143.

Bell, E. V. "Bankers Sign A Truce," *Current History,* XLI (December 1934), pp. 257-263.

Business Week. New York, 1930-1935.

Golembe, C. H. "The Deposit Insurance Legislation of 1933: An Examination of Its Antecedents and Its Purposes," *Political Science Quarterly,* LXXV (June 1960), pp. 181-200.

The Literary Digest. New York, 1932-1935.

Time. New York, 1932-1935.

NEWSPAPERS

The Journal of Commerce. (New York), 1932-1935.
The New York Times. 1932-1935.
The Wall Street Journal. 1932-1935.

INDEX

ABOUT THE AUTHOR

Helen M. Burns received her doctorate from New York University. She is Chief Law Librarian in the Law Library Division of the Federal Reserve Bank of New York, and previously served on the Maryland State Planning Commission.